KNOWING I'M SAVED

RICHARD FULTON

TRUE GRACE PUBLISHING

Copyright © 2018 Richard Fulton

All rights reserved.

ISBN: 978-1983249587

DEDICATION

To Jesus, the author and finisher of my faith. To C. H. Spurgeon, who led me to Jesus. To my wife, my children, and my church, who strengthened my hands, so I could write this book for Jesus.

CONTENTS

	Introduction	viii
1	Born In The Bible Belt	1
2	No Rest For The Weary	5
3	The Law Made Nothing Perfect	10
4	The Awakening	14
5	Where Do I Go From Here?	18
6	Oh To Grace How Great A Debtor!	23
7	He Was Despised And Rejected Of Men	28
8	So Close, Yet So Far Away	37
9	A Purpose For The Pain	40
10	I Don't Know If I'm Saved Or Lost	44
11	Understanding The Gospel	47
12	Getting Back To The Bible	52
13	The Sinner's Prayer	58
14	The Roman Road, Part I	65
15	The Roman Road, Part II	72
16	What If I'm Not One Of The Elect?	77
17	What Is Saving Faith?	82
18	What Is The Witness Of The Spirit?	90
19	The Unpardonable Sin	95

20	Do I Have To Know The Day I Was Saved?	100
21	Understanding Repentance	103
22	I Cannot Repent!	110
23	Do I Have To Do Good Works To Be Saved?	114
24	What If I Have Rejected Jesus Before	121
25	Do I Have To Be Baptized To Be Saved?	126
26	I Struggle To Believe!	131
27	What If God Is No Longer Dealing With My Heart?	137
28	The Devil's Treadmill	140
29	Conquering The Conflict Within You	144
30	Fruit Inspecting	149
31	Can I Lose My Salvation?	152
32	Letters From Others	157
33	Some Final Words	168

INTRODUCTION

"It is a fearful thing to fall into the hands of the living God" (Hebrews 10:31). There is no greater fear than the fear of being damned for your sin. There is no greater need than our need to be delivered from it. There is no greater love than the love Christ had when He faced our greatest fear. *"But God commends his love toward us, in that, while we were yet sinners, Christ died for us"* (Romans 5:8).

No matter how long you've doubted your salvation . . . no matter how bad you think your case may be, God loves you, and He will give you the help you need. God's love sent His Son to die for you, and His love sent me to point you to His Son. Struggling with the assurance of salvation is like being held in a dark and cruel dungeon. I know; I have been in that dungeon before. But there is a way out of it! And I wrote this book to show you the way.

Come with me then. Read my story. Watch me, as I go down into the dungeon where you are, and then come out with me as you watch God bring me out. By God's grace, you will learn the errors that created your doubt and find the answers to overcome it.

1 BORN IN THE BIBLE BELT

In a small 1970s Texas town, the average boy was sure to hear a little "hell, fire, and brimstone" preaching. But I was not your average boy. My father's side of the family belonged to the Church of God denomination. They attended an ultra-conservative church that began in my great-grandmother's home. Although I never knew my great-grandmother, I was told she was so modest that she kept her clothes on while taking a bath.

My mother's side of the family was not much different. Her parents belonged to the Independent Fundamental Baptist (IFB) denomination. The church they attended was so conservative it actually preached against the liberalism of other Baptist churches in town.

Between these two hardline denominations, my parents chose the Independent Fundamental Baptist church. This meant I would be attending Sunday morning, Sunday night, and Wednesday night services as a boy. It also meant I would be exposed to many zealous church workers growing up who would all have a part in shaping my early theology, forming the basis of my faith in God, and (most relevant to this book) my understanding of salvation.

In the church we attended, the gospel of Jesus Christ was presented as the church's greatest mission and as man's greatest need. The need for salvation was preached in the pulpit and taught in every classroom. God's coming judgment upon sinners was vividly described, leaving no doubt in my mind that sin was bad, hell was hot, and damnation will last forever. Continually hearing these things gave me a tender conscience and a constant fear of hell. In fact, being afraid of going to hell is one of my earliest childhood memories.

When I was about six years old, I was tired of living in fear. I didn't want to go to hell, and I was willing (and ready) to do anything to avoid it. Like many churches, our church had an "invitation" at the close of each service. During the invitation, people were invited to come to the front of the church to get spiritual help. One Sunday, I went to the front of the church and told my pastor I wanted to be saved. As was his custom, he summoned an "altar worker" to speak with me about my salvation. The altar worker was an older woman who worked with children my age. After speaking to my pastor, she had me kneel with her at the altar, where she asked me a few questions and ultimately led me in a "sinner's prayer" for salvation. I repeated the words to the prayer after her.

When I finished, she said, "Okay; you're saved now!" She told my pastor, and he joyfully announced to the church that I was saved.

Everybody was really happy about this, especially my mother. I can still remember her crying as she came down the aisle to meet me. Her tears confused me, so I asked the altar worker, "Why is my mother crying?"

"Because she's happy you got saved," she said.

I was baptized shortly thereafter, and this made me an official member of the church. To my family, this was a real cause for celebration. My grandmother even baked me a chocolate cake to commemorate the event. I saw this as a great time in my life—as a time when I could finally live out my childhood in confidence, without the fear of going to hell.

With this new confidence, I immersed myself in church activities. I sang in the choir, went on youth trips, and began telling others about their need to be saved as well. Feeling safe and secure, I continued this peaceful journey into adulthood.

But, once I turned eighteen, that peaceful journey came to an end. It had been twelve years since I knelt at the altar and prayed that prayer, and time had worn away the delicate details of my early childhood memories. As an adult, I could no longer remember the words I prayed, or what I was thinking when I prayed them.

I began to ask myself all sorts of questions. Did I really

understand salvation back then? Did I really have faith when I prayed at the altar? Or, was I just repeating words I was told to say?

These were serious questions, and I was the only one who could answer them. But, since I had no clear memory, I had no clear answers. Being unsure of what I did at the altar, I was now unsure that I was saved. This, of course, was the last thing I wanted. I wanted to know I was saved.

Looking for answers, I grabbed every gospel tract (pamphlet) I could find at our church, and I began reading them in private. I was hoping these tracts would give me some guidance, so I could settle the issue of my salvation once for all. After reading the tracts, I finally concluded that I was not saved. I determined that, as a child, I had repeated the words to a prayer, but I did not have the understanding I needed to be saved.

All the gospel tracts seemed to point me in the same familiar direction. After giving me the basic doctrines of salvation, they encouraged me to pray a sinner's prayer to be saved, just like the altar worker told me to do when I was six, and just like I had been telling other people to do for the past twelve years. So, the solution to my problem seemed simple enough: I would pray a sinner's prayer once again, and I would trust God to save me; only *this* time, I would be old enough to know what I was doing, and I would do it with all my heart!

So, at age eighteen, I knelt down once again, this time at the foot of my bed, and I prayed another sinner's prayer. I told God I knew I was a sinner, and that His Son, Jesus, died for my sins. I told God I wanted to be His child and go to heaven. And, with a sincere childlike faith, I asked God to save me right then and there, and I trusted Him to save me with all my heart.

When I finished praying, a wonderful feeling swept over me. It felt supernatural. It felt like a heavy load had been lifted off my chest. This euphoric feeling was real and undeniable, and I took it as confirmation from God that He had just saved me. Naturally, I was eager to tell my family, so I left my room and told them I had just been saved. Once again, they rejoiced. Once again, I was baptized. And, once again, I had peace that I was going to heaven.

Like before, I remained active in church as a young adult. I sang in the choir, drove a church bus, and I even began teaching children's church on Sunday mornings. I really seemed to be growing as a Christian, and I was growing in my personal life as well. I got married, went to college, and began pursuing my dream of becoming a Texas Highway Patrol Trooper.

In 1989, that dream became a reality, and I began my new career in law enforcement. This new career moved me to a new town, but it didn't take me long to find a new church home. Being true to my roots, I joined another Independent Fundamental Baptist church, and I really loved the people there. I also had the privilege of adding an extra person to the congregation, because my first daughter was born that same year.

So, within a few short months, I had a new job, a new church, a new town, and a brand-new baby. Life was unfolding quickly for me, and I was glad to be living it. Everything seemed to be on course for me to live a happy, normal, and productive Christian life.

But, what I didn't know was, my life would be far from happy and normal. God was about to use this special time in my life to accomplish a special work—to do something that, to this day, still amazes me. The people I would meet, and the things I would see, hear, and experience during this time, would all be part of the divinely different plan God had for me. The foreknowledge of God had cut a path for me that veered far from the main road, and l was predestined to take it. This path would take me through the habitations of devils, and through very dark, difficult, and lonely places. In the end, however, this unpleasant journey would be well worth the trip.

But, for the time being, I was a happy young man in every area of my life—my health, my family, and my career. But, most important of all, my salvation was secure, and I was on my way to heaven—or at least I thought.

2 NO REST FOR THE WEARY

Not long after I joined my new church, we had a guest preacher speak during one of our evening services. His sermon was on the rapture of the church and the great tribulation. In his message, he graphically described the horrific plagues that would come upon the earth in the last days and the impending doom that awaited sinners.

A lot of people were shouting "amen" that night, but I wasn't one of them. While others were braving the storm of his fiery sermon, I found no shelter in the sinner's prayer I prayed when I was eighteen. Like Noah's flood, it seemed as if I was standing outside the ark, and the words from that damning sermon were raining down upon me.

How did this happen to me? I was still in my early twenties. It had only been a few years since I knelt by my bed and asked God to save me. It felt as if a load had been lifted off my chest back then, but all I could feel now was dreadfulness, confusion, and fear. When I knelt by my bed at eighteen, I thought I had nailed down my salvation for good. Why, then, was I doubting it again?

My memory wasn't the problem this time. I remembered clearly what I did, prayed, and believed beside my bed that night. But I still had no peace—no peace in what *I did at the altar* when I was six, and no peace in what *I did by my bed* when I was eighteen.

After the service was over, my pastor was standing at the sanctuary exit with the guest preacher. They were greeting people as they left, and they were still talking about the sermon. I forced a smile on my face as I walked by.

My pastor reached out to shake my hand and said, "I'm sure glad I'm saved! I'd hate to be here after the rapture!"

Trying to appear confident, I verbally agreed with him, "Me too!" But I was absolutely miserable on the inside. I had no assurance of my salvation, and all I could think about was dying and going to hell.

After I got home, I stayed up all night, because I was too afraid to go to sleep. My bed felt like a trap door that could open any moment and drop me into hell. I really wanted to talk to my pastor that night, but I didn't want to wake him. So, I waited, and I prayed, wishing for the morning to come. And, when it finally came, I went to my pastor's house first thing to get some help.

In my pastor's home, I told him what I did at the altar when I was six, and what I did beside my bed when I was eighteen. But I told him that, in spite of what I had done, I was still not sure I was saved. Then I sat quietly to listen to his response.

I was eager to hear and do whatever he told me. I was determined to get some answers, and I was ready to settle this with God. I wasn't sure what my pastor would say, but I figured he would ask me a series of questions, and probe deep into my faith to see if it was genuine. Afterward, I figured he would diagnose my case and prescribe a remedy from God's Word.

But I was surprised by my pastor's response. He didn't ask me any probing questions; he didn't check to see if I had a clear understanding of the gospel, and he made no attempt to explain salvation to me. He just said I probably doubted my salvation because I wasn't being faithful enough to God. He told me if I read my Bible, prayed, and went to church more, then my doubts would probably go away. So, instead of probing me with questions, he loaded me with obligations.

Although this was not the response I expected, I trusted my pastor. So I left his home, and I did everything he told me to do. And, he was right: my doubts became weaker, and my confidence that I was saved became stronger.

So, it seemed like my pastor's recommendation was the perfect remedy. By performing these Christian duties, not only did my doubts become less severe, but I became more valuable to the church as well. On the surface, it looked like everybody had won. I had gained confidence in my salvation, and my pastor had gained a dedicated servant in the church.

This wonderful experience forged a strong bond between me and my pastor. He quickly became my friend and role model, and I quickly became his trusted "go to" person. My Christian life had never looked better, and I (once again) believed that I was saved. It's not that my doubts completely went away, but I had learned how to manage them. I had learned that, as long as I kept doing better, and kept trying harder, like my pastor said, I could keep the doubts under control.

As part of my Christian service, I began going out on visitation nights, inviting people in the community to come to church and telling them about their need to be saved. During visitation, my pastor and I would often team up. This gave me the opportunity to hear him talk to other people about their salvation. Since I still doubted my salvation from time to time, I would always listen closely to what he told them. Basically, he told people to do two things to be saved: 1. Surrender their lives to God, and 2. Ask God to save them.

What he said was agreeable to me—just surrender your life to God and ask Him to save you. This seemed simple enough, and those were two things I knew I had done. At that time in my life, I felt totally surrendered to God, and I had asked Him to save me many times. So, it seemed all my bases were covered.

According to my understanding of salvation, then, there were two things a man had to do to be saved: he had to turn from his sins in full surrender to God, and he had to ask God to save him. These two steps, therefore, became the basis of my confidence and the message I began sharing with others. The relationship I had with my pastor continued to grow stronger and stronger. He had won my confidence as a spiritual leader, and I had won his confidence as a disciple.

Eventually, my pastor approached me. "Brother Richard, I've noticed how much you've grown as a Christian, and I would like to recommend to the church that you be ordained as a deacon."

The thought of being a deacon was a little intimidating. I wasn't sure I was ready. But I trusted my pastor's judgment, so I gladly accepted his offer. Several months later, I was ordained, and I began my new role as a servant/leader in the church.

All this time, however, I still had those nagging doubts about my salvation lingering in the back of my mind. Trying to make sure

I was saved, I would often pray, "Lord, if I'm not saved, please save me." And, anytime I heard a preacher lead people in a sinner's prayer for salvation, I would always pray along silently, too, just in case. Time after time, I found myself praying these sinner's prayers, yet I could not find the assurance I longed for.

Nevertheless, the perceived advancements in my Christian life helped convince me that I was saved. And, as I continued in my zealousness for the things of God, my doubts were even more silenced by my pride. I began to view myself to be more righteous than my fellow church members. I also began taking a strong stand against sin, and I was especially good at pointing it out in the lives of other people. The grace of God will humble a man, but I was void of grace. Like the Pharisees, I had a zeal for God, but it was not according to knowledge (Romans 10:2).

With my pastor's mentoring, I blossomed into a good, rigid, fundamental Baptist. At which time, as if I had graduated to the next level, my pastor said to me, "Brother, I'm praying that God will call you to preach."

His statement shocked me. I had no desire to preach. Preaching was the furthest thing from my mind. I was a police officer, not a preacher. So, although I appreciated what he said, I basically laughed the idea off.

But my pastor wasn't laughing. From that point forward, every time he saw me, he would say, "I'm still praying that God will call you to preach."

His words carried a lot of weight with me. So, I naturally began to entertain the idea. I began to wonder if maybe this was indeed God's will for my life. I pondered the idea quite often, and I asked God to let me know.

Sometime later, at the close of one particular church service, I was pondering on whether or not God wanted me in the ministry. As I did, I had an extraordinary feeling sweep over me. There are really no words to describe this feeling, except that it felt supernatural and affirmative.

It was similar to the feeling I had when I knelt down by my bed at eighteen and asked God to save me. When this feeling swept over me, I believed in my heart that God was calling me to preach, just as my pastor had been praying. So, I went forward to inform my pastor, and he announced God's calling on my life to the church.

In time, I enrolled in seminary courses, and I began preaching whenever and wherever I could. I was a young, bold, and dynamic preacher. I always spoke with passion, and I was not afraid to speak out against sin.

The first sermon I preached was on the prodigal son. At the close of the message, people flocked down the isles to be saved, like I had never seen before in that little church. A total of six people made professions of faith that night. One of them was my pastor's daughter. In the eyes of me and my church, this strong and positive response to my first sermon was a confirmation that God had called me into the ministry.

My pastor wanted me to become an evangelist. So, yielding to his guidance, I set my heart toward an itinerant ministry. I had big plans of holding revivals across the nation, and I longed for the day when those big plans would become a reality.

But, along with those big plans, I still had a big problem—I was still struggling with recurring doubts about my salvation, and it was becoming more difficult for my zeal and Christian service to outrun them. When I told my pastor about this struggle, he said it was just the Devil trying to make me doubt. He said the Devil was attacking me more now because I was a preacher.

I told my pastor that I had repented of every sin that came to mind and that I had surrendered my whole life to God. I told him I didn't know what else to do. He told me there was nothing else I could do, and he assured me that it was normal for a Christian to doubt his salvation. In fact, my pastor said he once doubted his salvation so much that he woke up and thought he had missed the rapture. He said he was so afraid that he went to a cemetery to check the graves of some Christians he knew to make sure their bodies were still there.

Hearing that story didn't take my doubts away, but it made me feel better about having them. So I continued down the same path, serving God the best I knew how. I took seminary courses; I served in law enforcement, and I blamed every doubt I had on the Devil.

3 THE LAW MADE NOTHING PERFECT

Eventually, my service to God became exhausting. While trying to do what was good, I found something bad that I could not escape. It was the same depressing truth the apostle Paul had discovered in his own life, when he said, "*I find then a law, that, when I would do good, evil is present with me*" (Romans 7:21).

The more conscientious I became about living a godly life, the more I discovered how ungodly I really was. My pursuit of holiness made me increasingly aware of every little sin in my life. As the morning sun shines through a window, God's Word was shining brightly through the window of my heart, exposing all the filthy particles in the air that were previously unseen. No matter how hard I tried, I still saw my words, my thought life, and my devotion to God coming short of the standard God demanded and deserved.

I grew so sensitive to the presence of sin in my life that I felt I could not put one foot in front of the other without somehow sinning against God. Even the slightest infractions of God's law stung my conscience and condemned my soul. I hated to admit it, but I knew in my heart that, if I was God, I would surely condemn me for my sins, because I continued to commit the same ones over and over again. I was enslaved to sin, and I could not get free.

At times, it felt like the creation itself condemned me—like I was Cain, a fugitive and a vagabond in the earth. I became envious of animals, for they lived without fear of condemnation, while I lived in constant fear of it. I would have quickly traded places with a dog, or a lizard, for I would have rather lived as one of them, and returned to the ground, than to have lived as a man and gone to hell.

On my pastor's advice, I had been trying to live better and work harder for God. And this soothed my conscience for a while, but it could soothe it no longer. My efforts had finally reached their plateau. No matter how hard I tried to improve my life, *when I would do good, evil was present with me.*

I was absolutely miserable and thoroughly confused. What about the euphoric feeling I had when I asked God to save me at eighteen? What about the supernatural feeling I had when I surrendered to preach? Those feelings were real and powerful, and I could not deny them. But I also could not deny the continuing sense of my own condemnation, for it too was overwhelmingly real and powerful.

So, was I called by God? Or, was I condemned by God? I didn't know which to believe. Several people had professed salvation after hearing me preach, yet I didn't know if I was saved myself. How could I be torn between such two extremes? It seemed impossible, but this was the wretched position I was in.

While struggling with this great dilemma, I was asked to preach again at my church. This was a hard decision for me to make. If I was saved, I wanted to be faithful to my calling. But, if I was lost, I had no business preaching to others. Not knowing what else to do, and still holding out hope that I was a child of God who was battling the Devil, I agreed to preach, and I began studying for the message.

For my text, I chose Ezekiel 33:11: *"Say unto them, As I live, says the Lord GOD, I have no pleasure in the death of the wicked; but that the wicked turn from his way and live: turn you, turn you from your evil ways; for why will you die, O house of Israel?"*

I chose this text because it was something I could relate to. The prophet was told to say, *"turn you from your evil ways . . ."* And I had been turning from every evil way I knew.

But how could I preach to others in the condition I was in? I wanted to be a good preacher; I wanted to help others come to know God, but how could I give something to others that I wasn't sure I had myself? If I was truly saved, I didn't want to lose this battle with the Devil. I didn't want him to keep me from preaching what God had called me to preach. But, if I was lost, I didn't want to be the blind leading the blind.

I prayed hard for God to help me. I knew inside me that something was wrong, but I didn't know what to do about it. I only knew that I had turned from my evil ways, like my pastor told me, and that I had asked God to save me, like I read in the gospel tracts, and like I had heard in church all my life. Although I found no assurance in these things, they were all I had to hold on to. So I held on with all I had.

When it came time for me to preach, I was absolutely miserable. I still doubted my salvation, even as I walked up to the pulpit. My pastor could tell something was wrong. I'm sure he saw the misery on my face, and he looked unsure of what to do. But everyone knew I was supposed to preach, and they were waiting, so he went ahead and turned the service over to me.

It took all the strength I could muster to stand behind the pulpit that night. I felt like I was going to break down and be unable to deliver the message. But just the opposite took place. The moment I began to preach, all the fearful emotions inside me began spewing forth in a blistering fiery sermon. In my sense of desperation, I laid down the law like never before, beseeching everyone, *"turn you from your evil ways . . ."*

I gained a sense of relief from preaching that sermon. Oddly enough, condemning others has a strange way of easing your own conscience. Like the Pharisees, preachers sometimes fool themselves into thinking they can befriend the law by preaching it. But, *preaching* the law is different than *fulfilling* it.

The law of God is no respecter of persons. It accepts no form of bribe or flattery from any man. It demands full obedience from everyone, and it equally and justly condemns all who break it. So the law I had so passionately served that night gave me no rest for my labor. And the sinner's prayers I had so earnestly prayed from my youth gave me no reprieve from my guilt. When my sermon was over, I left the pulpit as miserable as I had come to it.

Nevertheless, the burning passion of my sermon did not go unnoticed. For, as soon as I stepped down from the pulpit, my pastor stood up and told the church it was evident God had called me to preach. He then called on the church to recognize God's calling on my life by licensing me as a minister of the gospel. The church agreed and, within a few short days, I was holding the certificate in my hand. So, there I was—a confused and miserable young man—with the church approving me, and the law condemning me.

4 THE AWAKENING

About eight o'clock one Wednesday evening, I was dispatched to a major crash on U.S. Highway 69. A young woman's car had overturned in the median. She had apparently become distracted while driving and allowed her vehicle to drift off the roadway. In the sudden shock of feeling her vehicle leave the roadway, she made a desperate attempt to steer it back onto the pavement. But, in her panicked response, she overcorrected her steering and caused it to roll over. Sadly, when her car rolled over, she suffered a head injury and died.

While I was investigating the crash, a passerby who knew the driver stopped. He told me she was a fine young woman, and that she had probably just left her Wednesday night church service. Based on what he told me, I didn't expect to find any drugs or alcohol in her system. But, since this was a fatal crash, I had to check.

After I finished up at the crash scene, I drove to the funeral home to collect a specimen of her blood. Since a dead person has no blood pressure, the funeral director had to draw the blood directly from her heart. To this day, I can still see her lying on that metal table. She was so young, in the prime of her life—just like me. I checked her driver's license. We were the same age. *That could be me lying there.*

Only the back of her head was injured. There wasn't a visible scratch on her body. She looked like she was sleeping. So, when the funeral director began pushing that long needle down into her chest, I felt like saying, "Stop! You'll hurt her!" But, I reminded myself, "She's not asleep, Richard; she's dead."

I continued looking on, watching the funeral director draw the lifeless blood from her heart. When his syringe was full, he pulled the needle back out of her chest and filled my evidence vial. As a young man, this was very sobering for me to watch. Once I received the vial back from him, I walked out of the funeral home, got back into my patrol car, and drove away with that young woman's blood.

It was late, and the dark and quiet highway afforded me time to think. While pondering the death of that young woman, the sense of my own mortality began to sink in. *I'm going to die, and I need to know the truth about religion and about where I will spend eternity.*

There are a lot of different religions out there. Even different "Christian" denominations argue over what it takes to be saved. What if my religion or denomination was wrong? And, if what I believed *was* wrong, how could I know what was true?

That night, I made a very important decision: I decided I would not gamble with my soul. I determined in my heart to study the different religions of the world, to make sure I was right, because *eternity is a long time to be wrong*. While driving down that road, I asked God to show me the truth. I told Him, "I don't care what religion I have, as long as I have you."

I didn't question the existence of God. I knew there was a God. I knew I didn't get here by accident. In my job as a state trooper, I had seen plenty of accidents. And I knew accidents could *take* life, but they could never *give* life. I knew accidents didn't create construction and order; they caused destruction and disorder.

I knew someone designed this marvelous world and made everything in it (including me) *on purpose*. And it seemed reasonable to me that if God made this world on purpose, He would naturally want to reveal Himself to His creation. How else would the creature know the purpose of its Creator?

I refused the notion of self-enlightenment. Whether it was Greek mythology, Buddhism, or Hinduism, the whole idea of men generating their own ideas about the afterlife, or inventing gods from their own imagination, was utter foolishness to me. A dark heart can no more fill itself with light than a dry well can fill itself with water. No, I knew there had to be some external source of truth, some divine repository from which the well of knowledge is supplied. I knew that, as rain comes from the ocean, so truth must come from God.

So, I didn't want the ideas of men; I wanted the words of God. I wanted to know what God Himself had to say to me, and I wanted to see it for myself. There are a limited number of books that claim to be divinely inspired, and I had to know which one was true.

Did God reveal Himself to us in the Koran? Did He use the book of Mormon? Did God speak to us through the Bible? And, if He did, did He use only the Old Testament, or did He speak through the New Testament too?

I decided the only way to answer this difficult question was to study the different religions and learn what each had to say. So, I began studying any religion that claimed to be divinely inspired, such as Islam, Judaism, and the different offshoots of Christianity.

Like searching for the proverbial "needle in a haystack," one would think searching for truth in a haystack of religions would prove to be a difficult task. But I found that my search for truth was surprisingly simple. Out of all the religions and so-called "Christian" denominations I studied, I quickly found they all had one thing in common: they all had a set of rules for me to keep. And, though each set of rules was different, they all basically formed the same moral law (love God, do good to others, etc.). And each group claimed that if I could keep its set of rules (its law) well enough, then God would accept me.

Amazingly, I found even the self-enlightened religions taught the same thing. Buddhism and Hinduism, for example, both teach karma, which claims that the sum of a person's actions decides his or her fate in a future existence. So, no matter what religion I studied, they all basically said the same thing.

Whether it was the Ten Pillars of Islam, the Ten Commandments of the Bible, or the karma of the heathen, every religion I studied essentially pointed me back to the same trap I was already in. No matter which set of rules I chose, they all told me to keep working, to keep trying, to keep doing my very best, and then maybe, hopefully, one day I might make it.

Thus, I came to realize that, regardless of the religion's name, or its country of origin, all religions were essentially the same. They were just one religion wrapped in different packaging. No matter what the package looked like on the outside, once the wrapping was removed, it was still a religion that was based on *me*—my undependable, feeble, and fallible performance. A performance which I knew fell miserably short of God's perfect standard.

So, I found that the religious "haystack" was actually a single straw of hay. And this made the golden needle of truth—the gospel of Jesus Christ—easy for me to find.

Regardless of how it was wrapped, religion offered me no hope, but when I laid down the golden needle of the gospel next to that religious straw, I found a glorious hope and a glaring difference between the two. In my quest for truth, I found that every religion in this world was based on *my* performance—what I must do for God—but the gospel was based on *Christ's* performance, what He had done for me. What genius! What marvelous wisdom I saw in this!

My best efforts fell short of God's standards. I was a sinner; I was unacceptable to God. But, through the gospel, God had made a way for me to be accepted by Him on the merit of another person—the Lord Jesus Christ. This was the golden needle of truth I had discovered.

I was now convinced that the Bible was God's Word to man and that the gospel was man's only way to God. Outside the gospel of Jesus Christ, there simply was no other way for me—an unrighteous man—to be accepted by a righteous God.

Ever since I was a child, I had always believed Jesus died for my sins and rose again. But after studying all those different religions, the person of Jesus Christ, and most especially His death on the cross, took on a whole new meaning to me. For, I now understood the *cross* to be the one thing that separates the gospel from all other (false) religions. The cross distinguishes between those who live and those who die. Those without the cross have no hope of life, but those with the cross have no fear of death.

5 WHERE DO I GO FROM HERE?

I was so thankful God answered my prayer. Satan had spun a tangled web of religion for me, but God answered my prayer and graciously divided the light from the darkness in my mind. God confirmed to me that the Bible was His Word to man. But, most importantly, He showed me that Jesus was the only way of salvation, and that His cross was the only remedy for my sin. The cross made me realize that any "Christian" denomination requiring "good works" to be saved (or stay saved), was just a false religion, deceitfully wrapped in a "Christian" package.

As I said before, I had always heard about the cross growing up, but my study of the different religions made me realize how important it was. I realized that if I could get what Christ did on the cross credited to my account, then I would surely be saved. For, how could God punish Jesus for my sins, and then punish me for those same crimes? That would be double jeopardy.

As a state trooper, I routinely searched the judicial dockets on every charge I filed. When a person failed to appear in court on one of my traffic citations, for example, the judge would issue a warrant for his or her arrest. I would then find that person and put him or her in jail. But, if the person's fine was paid, then the law was satisfied. There was nothing more I could do. I had no power to make an arrest in that case.

When I examined the court dockets, I could see the names of every person I cited and the charges I had filed against them. And, when a person's fine was paid, the judge would always draw a big

"X" across his or her place on the docket, crossing out the charges I had filed against them. Near the center of the "X," the judge would write the word "Paid."

The moment that "X" was made, the charge was settled forever, and it could never be brought against that person again. It didn't matter *who* paid the fine. Parents, for example, routinely paid fines for their children, because they had no ability to pay themselves. This did not matter to the court, and it did not matter to me; the only thing that mattered was that the law was satisfied—the penalty had been paid.

That is why I needed the cross. I knew Jesus died there to pay the penalty for my sin, and I wanted God to apply His cross to my docket. I wanted God to draw a big "X" across all my sins and mark them "Paid" by the blood of Jesus Christ.

I had never understood the cross like this before. Up until this time, I had always viewed the cross as something Jesus had to do so God could "save me" when I asked Him. And I had asked Him to save me over and over again.

But I now realized that Jesus' death on the cross—not the sinner's prayer—was the centerpiece of the gospel message. I didn't need "Prayed" written on my docket; I needed "Paid" written on my docket. For, only the full payment of my penalty could blot out my crimes in heaven's court and settle my case forever.

Now that I understood this, only one thing mattered to me: I had to get what Jesus did on the cross credited to my account. But, the problem was, I didn't know how to do this. Unlike earthly courts, God's court had no papers for me to sign, or an office for me to appear in. I was like a starving man, and the cross was my food. But I didn't know how to get Jesus' death to my mouth and into my belly so I could live.

I was so distraught and confused, and I prayed earnestly for God to give me this understanding. One day, in my garage, I fell on my face before God, and I poured my heart out to Him, begging Him to help me . . . begging Him to show me what to do. I prayed so hard that, when I finally opened my eyes, I saw a big puddle of tears on the cement floor.

As I stared at that puddle, I began to wonder. *God, don't you love me? Don't you care about me? I know you want people to be saved. So, what's wrong with me? Why is this so hard for me?*

In my search for peace, I grew desperate for answers that my church could not give. My continual barrage of questions exhausted the pastoral staff, and their answers left me none the wiser. So I decided to look for help outside my church.

I began calling, writing, and visiting pastors both far and near, hoping one of them could help me. Out of all the preachers I spoke to, I still couldn't get the answers I needed. Instead of clearing up my confusion, most gave me poor counsel and empty words, which proved incapable of helping me.

One preacher told me, "I believe the Holy Spirit is telling me you are saved."

Another preacher said, "You keep bouncing that ball down, Brother, and one day it won't bounce back up."

And another preacher told me to just repeat my "sinner's prayer" again to be sure I was saved.

Though I appreciated their willingness to help, their words were like empty bandages being applied to infected wounds by physicians who had no medicine. So I began searching for more meaningful and substantial answers. I didn't want a mysterious gospel I couldn't understand. I wanted a clear gospel I could see and comprehend. I wanted a tangible gospel I could put my arms around and make my own.

Finding no help from the preachers of my time, I decided to read old books, written by preachers from an earlier generation, to hear what they had to say about salvation. So, I went to the local Christian bookstore, and I asked for the oldest books they had. I wanted to see how the gospel was preached at an earlier time in history when its presentation and doctrines were still pure.

What I didn't realize was, the gospel has been perverted by men since the day God gave it to them. The first son of Adam and Eve (Cain) polluted the gospel by placing unacceptable gifts upon his altar. And a great percentage of the New Testament epistles, which were written to the early church, were dedicated to correcting, rebuking, and warning the saints about the many perversions of the gospel that had already begun. So, instead of giving me the clear answers I was looking for, some of the books I read brought me into greater confusion and despondency.

My struggle and my perplexity were beyond words. One particular night, I read John 7:37-38, *'In the last day, that great day of the feast, Jesus stood and cried, saying, If any man thirst, let him come unto me, and drink. He that believeth on me, as the scripture hath said, out of his belly shall flow rivers of living water."*

A commentary on that passage said that if I was "thirsty" for salvation, then I should "drink." I know now what the writer meant, but I was so desperate and confused back then that I actually physically swallowed, trying to be saved—trying to somehow get Christ's payment and salvation for myself, trying to get my crimes crossed out in heaven's docket. What I needed was plain speech. I needed someone to explain how to be saved to me in words I could understand.

Furthermore, some of the old literature I read was written by Calvinists, who claimed it was God's will to send some people to heaven and to condemn the rest to hell. According to Calvinists, it is God's will to be merciful to only a limited number of people but to deny salvation to everyone else. They believe God does not deny salvation to people because they reject Him, but because God has chosen to not save them.

According to Calvinists, the people God wants to be saved are His "elect," and the people God does not want to be saved are the "non-elect." But, most frightening of all, Calvinists claim that Jesus only died for the sins of the elect, and thus salvation is only available to them. They claim we're either one of God's elect or we're not, and that we have no ability to choose which group we want to be in.

Since I was having so much trouble obtaining salvation, I began to wonder if maybe I wasn't one of God's elect. *Has this been my problem the whole time? Was I not chosen to be saved?* The thought of being rejected by God and condemned to hell, with no ability to choose God's forgiveness, was horrifying to me.

To make matters worse, the Devil began to assault my mind with the most hideous thoughts about God, which caused me to believe I might have committed the unpardonable sin—blasphemy against the Holy Spirit. There are no words to express the anguish I was in. God's court seemed to call for my condemnation, and my own conscience mournfully agreed.

The thought of me going to hell became so real, and my fear of hell became so horrific. It seemed that my life on earth was now intolerable. I had two precious little children at the time, and my mind was racing. *Richard, you are unable to give your children the most important thing they need. If you can't figure out how to be saved for yourself, how can you share it with your children?*

    The Devil tempted me to commit suicide. He reminded me about Judas, who, after he betrayed Christ, went out and hung himself. The Devil told me, "Since you're going to hell anyway, you might as well go now and get it over with."

    Moreover, I didn't want my children to go to hell. And I reasoned in my mind that if I were to kill myself, then my wife could marry a real Christian, and maybe he could lead my children to Christ. That is how miserable and hopeless I was.

6 OH TO GRACE HOW GREAT A DEBTOR!

I feared my misery would never end. But, one night, by God's providence, my situation took a sudden turn for the better. A civilian friend of mine was riding with me in my patrol car. As my shift was about to end, my friend told me about a book he had recently read by Charles H. Spurgeon, a famous pastor back in the 1800s. My friend said he really enjoyed the book, because Pastor Spurgeon explained salvation so well and made it easy for him to understand.

My friend was unaware of my struggle, but his description of that book really got my attention. It sounded exactly like what I had been looking for. I told my friend I wanted to borrow the book.

"Sure; I'll bring it to you one of these days," he said.

"No; I want to borrow the book *tonight*." I insisted.

My friend seemed surprised by my eagerness to read the book. He was willing to loan it to me that night. But, he had so many books, he wasn't sure if he could find it. So, I drove my friend to his house. And, as he went inside to look, I prayed that he would find it.

Moments later, by the grace of God, he came out with the book in his hand. I was so thankful God let him find it. I took it from him and immediately drove home to read it. The name of the book was *All of Grace*.

It was late at night, but I could hardly put the book down. For the first time in my life, I read the gospel as it was intended to be told. When Pastor Spurgeon shared the gospel, he did something for me no other pastor had done before: *he pointed me away from myself.*

He pointed me away from my "sinner's prayers," away from my surrendered life, away from anything I could do or say to be saved. I was pointed away from anything about me. And he pointed toward what Jesus *had already accomplished on my behalf.*

Like a skillful surgeon, Pastor Spurgeon took the scalpel of scripture and removed the cancerous tissue of false "Christianity" from my heart. He then sewed me back up with the thread of God's promise and encouraged me to apply the healing ointment of the cross.

I knew the cross was what I needed. But still, I did not know how to apply it. Besides, I wasn't sure if I was one of God's elect. How could I know God wanted *me* to be saved?

As I continued to read Spurgeon's book, I found some relief when he introduced me to Romans 5:6: *"For when we were yet without strength, in due time Christ died for the ungodly."*

Christ died for the ungodly. What glorious words! In all my confusion, if there was one thing I knew for certain, it was that I was ungodly. Therefore, if Christ died for the *ungodly*, then Christ surely died for *me!* In those priceless words, *"Christ died for the ungodly,"* I knew my fine had been paid to heaven's court, and I knew heaven's Judge wanted me to be saved. It was simple enough: the penalty for sin is death, and Jesus died to pay that penalty for me: *the ungodly.*

Now assured of God's good will toward me, I no longer feared Calvinism or the doctrine of election. By those words, *"Christ died for the ungodly,"* I knew God loved me, and He didn't want me to go to hell. For, God would not have sent His Son to pay my penalty if He wanted to condemn me. John 3:17 says, *"For God sent not his Son into the world to condemn the world; but that the world through him might be saved."*

I was certain God sent His Son to pay the penalty for my sin— to satisfy heaven's court for the crimes I'd committed. Yet, how to apply Jesus' payment to my account was still a mystery to me. I'd been studying, praying, and even begging God to show me what I must do to make this needful application, but I still did not know how.

"Christ died for the ungodly." The payment for my sin had been

rendered to the Judge, but I didn't know how to act upon this information and officially settle my case in heaven's court. But, as I continued reading, the scales began to fall from my eyes: Christ's death on the cross was not only *for* my salvation; His death *was* my salvation! Therefore, *if I could be sure that Christ died for my sins on the cross, then I could be sure that I was saved.* Pastor Spurgeon revealed this to me when he said,

> Hold you on to this one fact—*"In due time Christ died for the ungodly."* This truth will not require from you any deep research or profound reasoning, or convincing argument. There it stands: *"In due time Christ died for the ungodly."* Fix your mind on that, and rest there.

These words rang true to my heart, but they were so foreign to my ears. Could salvation really be that simple? Could I merely fix my mind on the wonderful truth that Christ died in my place, and simply rest on that fact? I knew from God's Word that we were saved by "faith." But, I had never understood faith this way before.

Up until this time, I had always understood faith to mean that I was supposed to trust God to "save me" when I asked Him to. I had seen faith as something I had to sort of conjure up in order to "get saved," and I was never sure I had enough of it. But Pastor Spurgeon explained faith differently.

He said faith was taking God at His word—*believing* Him. In other words, instead of trusting Jesus to do something to me (when I asked), I needed to simply take God at His word and trust what He said Jesus had already done for me (on the cross). What an incredible difference this made for me. For the first time in my life, I didn't see salvation as something I had to beg for in the present, but as something I had to believe Christ did for me in the past! *Christ died for the ungodly.* What more need I be told?

If Christ died for me, then my penalty was already paid at the cross. It seemed reasonable, therefore, that I needed only to believe it. I pondered deeply on this for some time, and I marveled that salvation could be as simple as me taking God at His word concerning this wonderful truth.

What Christ accomplished on the cross was, to me, the most coveted possession a man could have, and I desperately wanted it. Speaking of what Christ did there, Pastor Spurgeon said, *"Christ died for the ungodly* . . . Let this one great, gracious, glorious fact lie in your spirit till it perfumes all your thoughts . . ."

And that's what I did. I continued to think on the glorious fact that Christ died for me until it flooded all my thoughts. As I thought about Jesus on the cross, my mind's eye carried me away to Calvary, and I could visualize Him dying there. In my imagination, I saw His bleeding and broken body nailed to the tree, dying for me, *the ungodly*. I saw Him crushed beneath the heavy burden of my sin, enduring the full weight of my condemnation, as He struggled to take each breath.

As I contemplated on these thoughts, I began to see the cross as the Scriptures described it. And, when I looked upon it, I no longer saw the sin of the *world* on Jesus; I saw *my* sin on Jesus. And, I saw the wrath of God poured out on Him for the crimes I had committed. By faith, I saw Jesus suffering all the hell I feared, and I saw how every sin that could put me in hell had been put on Him.

God had marked a big "X" on heaven's docket, crossing out the charges against me with the death and blood of His Son, forever settling my case! Being so desirous to claim this wonderful truth for myself, I sort of wrapped my arms around Jesus and His cross, and I clung to that for dear life. I remember saying, "This is my only hope, God. My only hope for heaven is what Jesus did for me."

It was little more than a sheer act of desperation. As a drowning man would cling to a piece of driftwood, so I clung to the only hope I had—the cross. And, as I clung to it, God graciously opened my eyes, for I suddenly realized that this was what it meant to believe in Jesus Christ.

Believing in Christ meant I was to take God at His word, making the good news (the gospel) of Jesus and His cross my only hope for heaven. I had finally done that. Now the promise of eternal life belonged to me, for, Jesus said in John 3:18, *"He that believes in him is not condemned . . ."*

The best way I can describe my faith in Jesus is with a game called "Hide and Seek" that I played as a child. In that game, several of us kids would hide while a designated person (the seeker) counted to a certain number. As soon as the seeker reached that number, he would begin searching for the hidden children. If he found and touched one of the children, that child would lose the game.

But, somewhere on the playground, there was a safe place the kids could run to. That place was called "base." Usually "base" was a tree (or something large) we could run to and touch. And the object of the game was for us to touch base before the seeker could touch us. If we could make it to base, we were safe. We won the game. We were "home free".

Like the "seeker" in the game, God's Ten Commandments sought me out, for I was guilty of breaking them. We are all *ungodly*, and because of this, God's law will soon lay hold of us and condemn us for our crimes. But, the good news (gospel) is, *"Christ died for the ungodly."* In God's great love for us, He has designated the cross as "base." And if we will run to the cross and lay hold of Jesus, we will be safe (saved). We will be "home free".

There is only one base. If a child went to any another object than base, even if he or she mistakenly ran to the wrong tree, then that child was not safe. In the same way, the cross is the only refuge God has given us to run to. It is the only object we can put our hand of faith on and be saved.

This had been my problem all along. Instead of running to the cross, I had run to my sinner's prayers, to my religion, to my ministry, to my trips down to the "altar," to my devotion to God, and to my religious duties. I ran to what *I did for Jesus* when I should have run to what *Jesus did for me*. The apostle Paul, wanting to make sure the Corinthian people knew which object was base, told them, in 1 Corinthians 2:2, *". . .I determined not to know anything among you, except Jesus Christ, and him crucified."*

Perhaps this is your problem right now. Perhaps you have missed base and put your hand on the wrong object. If your hand is on anything other than the cross where Jesus died, then you need to let go of it and lay hold of nothing else, *"except Jesus Christ, and him crucified."*

Christ died for the ungodly. Just take God at His word concerning this wonderful truth. Believe in the Savior who died in your place, for *He that believes in him is not condemned.*

7 HE WAS DESPISED AND REJECTED OF MEN

Having finally understood the gospel, I knew I had to inform my pastor of the great discovery I had made. I had to tell him about the faith and peace I had found in the cross of Christ. But I knew telling him would be difficult to do.

When people found out that I, the preacher, had just become a Christian, I would no doubt become quite a spectacle. My preaching, and my service as a deacon, would also have to cease. Some of the things I had been taught were wrong, and I needed to step down, so I could start over, and (this time) learn the Bible correctly, from the ground up.

I wasn't ashamed of my new faith in Jesus, but I knew this change would put me in an awkward position. Nevertheless, awkward or not, telling my pastor was the right thing to do, so I drove to his home, and I told him that I had just been saved.

"What do you mean you just got saved?" my pastor asked.

"Brother, the best way I can explain it to you is like this: All these years, I had done everything I knew to do to be saved—everything, that is, except trust the One who had done everything for me already."

My pastor was visibly upset. He had been promoting my ministry to the church; he told them he sensed God's call on my life. Now everyone would know he had been endorsing a lost person. I suppose he feared this would cause people to question his discernment as a pastor.

Instead of being glad that I finally had assurance of my salvation, my pastor seemed more concerned about protecting his reputation. "Okay, here's what I want you to do. At the next service, I want you to take your deacon ordination certificate and your preaching license, and I want you to walk down to the front of the church and lay them on the altar. Then, I want you to tell the congregation that you have been living a lie and that you have been pretending this whole time."

Up to this time, I had always followed my pastor's counsel, but I couldn't follow it this time. I told my pastor I could not say the things he wanted me to say, because they weren't true. He knew how hard I had sought the truth from him, and he knew how many times I had gone to him for help and followed his advice. I had been deceived, and I had been ignorant, but I was no pretender. Like Saul of Tarsus, I'd had *"a zeal of God, but not according to knowledge"* (Romans 10:2).

The next service, therefore, I simply informed the church that I was recently saved, and I was now resting in what Jesus accomplished for me on the cross. In front of the congregation, my pastor questioned me about the timing of my salvation, as if he was skeptical about my new profession of faith. But I stood firm, because I knew the truth, and I knew the Savior whom I believed.

After announcing my salvation to the church, I stepped down from any ministry position I once held, and I dedicated myself to prayer, to the study of God's Word, and to private Christian service. I was thankful for my salvation, but I was exhausted from the long spiritual battle I had endured. I needed rest. The publicity and the circumstances in which my conversion took place also left me somewhat embarrassed. Consequently, I wanted to serve God behind the scenes and never be in the public eye again.

Although I was now saved, I was still weak and unsettled on a lot of issues. Taking advantage of my weakness, the Devil continued to harass me, trying his best to overthrow my faith in Christ and to distort my understanding of the gospel. His unrelenting attacks, along with the life-long struggle I had already endured, made me want a perfect understanding of the gospel more than anything.

I wanted to be strong in the faith, not just for myself, but for others, too. So, one particular afternoon, I bowed my knees, and I asked God to give me a deep and solid understanding of the gospel. I told God I wanted to know the gospel, and the way of salvation, "inside and out."

The Lord responded to my prayer by giving me a great hunger for the Scriptures, and by opening my eyes little by little to a greater understanding of the gospel as I read them. In addition, the Lord furnished me with some excellent Bible teaching by way of a local Christian radio station, whose broadcasts helped me immensely.

I also received much help from a missionary in Indonesia, who, having learned of my desire to understand the gospel better, mailed me the curriculum he used to teach the gospel to unreached tribal people in that country. The wonderful teaching plan he used taught the gospel chronologically from "Creation to Christ," causing me to understand the gospel from a whole Bible perspective.

By these three things—my personal study, the radio broadcasts, and the "Creation to Christ" material—my roots began to sink deeper into the gospel. The more I grew in the grace of Jesus, however, the more discrepancies I found between the gospel I now believed and the gospel I was hearing at my church. I believed in a gospel based entirely on the work of Jesus—what He did, but my church was preaching a "gospel" that was based (at least in part) on the work of men—what they did.

Though my church claimed salvation was by grace through faith and not of works, they, nevertheless, preached a gospel that contained works. When my pastor told someone how to be saved, for example, he would usually tell him or her to "surrender your life to God and ask God to save you." Before I was saved, this sounded reasonable and biblical to me.

But, now that I had come to Christ, I knew this was contrary to what the Bible teaches. Salvation is not about us giving *our* life to God; it's about Christ giving *His* life for us. Salvation is not about *asking* God to do something *to* us; it's about *trusting* God for what He (in Christ) has already done *for* us on the cross.

One day, before I was saved, I was in my pastor's study when he received a voicemail on his phone. It was a sad message left by a Baptist pastor from another town. The pastor said his son needed to be saved, and he asked my pastor to meet with his son (who lived near our church) and lead him to the Lord. My pastor immediately called the other pastor's son, and he agreed to come to the church and meet with us.

When the pastor's son walked in, I recognized him as a police officer from a nearby town. His name was Eric. As my pastor spoke with Eric about his life, and about his need to be saved, Eric was both honest and humble. He told my pastor he had not been living the life he should, and that he needed to be saved.

"Well, I believe you know what you need to do Eric," my pastor said

"Yes, sir."

My pastor told Eric to get down on his knees and tell God he was sorry. He told him to surrender his life to God and ask God to save him.

Eric, with an earnest and tearful prayer, bowed his knees and confessed his sins to God. Eric told God he was sorry. Eric told God he was now surrendering his life to Him, and Eric asked God to forgive him and to save him. When Eric finished praying, my pastor and I rejoiced.

But, after I was saved, I realized Eric never heard the gospel from my pastor. In my pastor's study, Eric had surrendered his life, confessed his sins, bowed his knees, and asked God to forgive him and to save him. That's what *Eric* had done, but where was *Jesus* in all of that?

Where was Jesus' life? Where was Jesus' death? Where was Jesus' resurrection from the grave? Apart from faith in a crucified Savior, Eric's "salvation" had a form of godliness on the outside, but it was powerless and empty on the inside.

After I was saved, I happened to see Eric one day at the county jail. Fearing he was still lost, my heart longed to speak with him. I wanted to tell Eric what I had learned about Jesus. I wanted to make sure he understood the gospel and had assurance of his salvation. So, I approached him privately.

"Eric, did you ever get the matter of your salvation settled?"

"I'm glad you asked me that, Richard. I need to talk to you. I'm confused, and I don't know if I'm saved."

I knew right then that God must have arranged this meeting between us. Eric had a religious background. His father was a pastor, and he had spoken to my pastor as well. Yet, like me, Eric's religious training and experience had left him confused.

Neither his father nor my pastor would've intentionally misled Eric. And I know my pastor would have never intentionally misled me. But, clearly, there had to be something wrong with the method of evangelism we were exposed to. Somewhere down the line, there must have been a breakdown in the way our churches were communicating the "gospel."

Instead of taking Eric to the New Testament and giving him another prayer to pray (as is commonly done), I did something different: I took Eric to the first book of the Bible. And, following the natural order of the Bible, I carefully worked my way from Genesis to Jesus, explaining the gospel to Eric, and showing him how salvation worked.

I showed Eric how the human race (in Adam) fell into sin in the garden of Eden, and how God had warned Adam and Eve that the penalty for their sin would be death. But I showed Eric how God lovingly laid the sins of Adam and Eve onto innocent animal substitutes and killed the animal substitutes instead of them. I then showed Eric how God clothed Adam and Eve with the skins of those innocent animals, as described in Genesis 3:21, *"Unto Adam also and to his wife did the LORD God make coats of skins, and clothed them."*

I explained to Eric that, by clothing Adam and Eve in the skins of the innocent animals that died for them, God was illustrating for them (and for us) how He would one day clothe us in the innocence of Jesus who would die for us. Furthermore, I showed him how Abel (believing God's promise to send a Savior) also offered to God an innocent animal substitute, and how God accepted Abel on the basis of the animal that died in his place, as mentioned in Genesis 4:4, *"And Abel, he also brought of the firstlings of his flock and of the fat thereof. And the Lord had respect unto Abel and to his offering..."*

Finally, I explained how the salvation of Jesus Christ, who died in the place of sinners, was illustrated over and over again throughout the Old Testament by the continual animal sacrifices that were offered by the priests for the sins of the people, and how Jesus fulfilled all these sacrifices when He offered up Himself.

Then I said, "Eric, just as God clothed Adam in the innocence of the animal that died for him, and, just as God accepted Abel on account of the animal that died for him, so God will accept you and clothe you in the innocence of Jesus who died in your place. This is the good news (gospel) of what Jesus has done for you. So, if you will accept Jesus, Eric, then God will accept you."

After I finished the gospel story, I didn't ask Eric to do anything. I didn't give him a prayer to pray, and I didn't tell him to surrender his life to God. Jesus had done it all, and there was nothing left for Eric to do. I simply explained the gospel, then I stopped, and I waited for his response.

This was new for me, so I wasn't sure how he would respond. But, his reaction made a real and permanent impact on my spiritual life. I will never forget it.

With a solemn look on his face, Eric responded with a strange combination of both bewilderment and delight in his voice. "Richard, nobody has ever told me that before. I have never heard this in my life. This is wonderful! You have got to share this with my wife. She really needs to hear this."

For the average churchgoer, Eric's story would be hard to understand. Most would be surprised that someone like Eric, whose father was a pastor, and who had recently spoken to my pastor, could still, after hearing the gospel from me, claim he had never heard it until now. But, sadly, it was no surprise to me.

2 Kings 22:8 recounts the story of when the Bible got lost in the house of God. And, sadly, just as the Word of God once got lost in the house of God, so the gospel of Jesus Christ has been lost in many churches. In fact, throughout my evangelistic ministry, I have had the privilege of sharing the gospel with many lost church members. And, like Eric, time and time again, many have told me: "I've never heard this before."

Think about the significance of these words. The single most important mission of the church is to preach the gospel of Jesus Christ. But, if our own church members are not hearing and comprehending it, then we have a real problem. How did we get here? How did this happen to us?

As the serpent cunningly introduced the lie to Eve, so Satan introduced cleverly altered versions of the gospel to our modern churches. Because they were so similar to the true gospel, their falsity was hardly noticed, and many church leaders approved them. Now that they have gained widespread acceptance in many circles, they have diluted and distorted the message of salvation, even to the point in which the gospel is no longer heard in many churches.

This subtle corruption of the gospel is an old tactic of the Devil. A good example can be found in Paul's letter to the church of Galatia, where a corrupt version of the gospel had been introduced to this otherwise solid group of believers. Paul wrote to condemn that corrupt version. Listen to what Paul told them in Galatians 1:6-7: *"I marvel that you are so soon removed from him that called you into the grace of Christ unto another gospel: Which is not another; but there be some that trouble you, and would pervert the gospel of Christ."*

Ever since the garden of Eden, Satan has been corrupting and counterfeiting the gospel of Jesus Christ. So, until Jesus comes again, every generation of believers will experience the corruption of the gospel message. As a result, every generation will face its own unique challenges to the gospel that it will have to overcome. So, regardless of what decade or century you read this book in, this truth will remain: *"there be some that trouble you, and would pervert the gospel of Christ."*

Notice the words *"trouble you"* and *"pervert the gospel"* in the above text. The people in the Galatian church were troubled because there were some among them who had perverted the gospel of Christ. Thus, when it comes to the assurance of our salvation, we learn a very important truth here. Namely, where the gospel is perverted, there will be people who are troubled.

In my evangelistic ministry, I've had countless people contact me regarding their assurance of salvation. These people have ranged anywhere from minor children to senior adults, from manual laborers to business owners, and from Bible college students to educated senior pastors. And, in most every instance, their lack of assurance was due to some fundamental misunderstanding they had about the gospel. Once again, where the gospel is perverted, there will be people who are troubled.

In my church, people were told to do two things to be saved: Surrender your life to God and ask Him to save you. This sounds good on the surface. But, as good as it may sound, it is not the gospel. Remember, Paul said, *"For I determined not to know any thing among you, except Jesus Christ, and him crucified."*

The problem with my pastor's two-step gospel was that it side-stepped the cross of Jesus Christ. Instead of not knowing anything *except Jesus Christ, and Him crucified*, this two-step gospel left people knowing everything but Jesus Christ and Him crucified, for the sacrifice of Jesus was hardly (if ever) mentioned.

You can surrender your life to God and ask Him to save you, and still never trust in the sacrifice of Jesus Christ. And, sadly, with "gospel" messages like this, that's what people sometimes do.

Ultimately, therefore, I had to confront my pastor about the "gospel" message at our church. As kindly as I could, I had to explain to him how his message had caused me (and others) so much confusion.

When I confronted him, I told him we needed to preach the cross of Jesus Christ. And I asked him what biblical authority he had to tell people they could be saved by "surrendering" their lives to God. Of course, there was no biblical support for the two-step "gospel" he preached. Nevertheless, he stood his ground and grew weary with my defense of the gospel. He was irritated by my belief that we are not saved by what we give to God but by faith in what God gave for us (Jesus).

Ultimately, my stand for the gospel caused my pastor to have a complete disdain for me. He, who once was my best friend, and who had once promoted me in the church, had now, on account of my faith in Christ, become my worst enemy and critic. He saw my passion for the gospel as a threat to his ministry, and he wanted me to leave the church.

Standing in the pulpit one night, he brought a loud and angry sermon against me. I can still hear him now, yelling at me from the pulpit: "Please leave this church!" As soon as his "sermon" was over, I left his church, and I never went back.

Because of the gospel, people in that church who once supported me, now turned their backs on me. One man, a beloved missionary friend of mine in the church, called me as soon as he heard the news of my departure. He had a question to ask me.

"Brother Richard, I only want to know one thing."

"Sure, Brother Don. What is it?"

"Did you *pray* when you got saved?"

"No, Sir. I didn't."

"Well, that's what they told me, but I just had to hear it for myself. I'm glad you're gone. You don't believe like us, so you don't belong with us."

I'm glad you're gone. People sometimes think I split hairs when it comes to my defense of the gospel. I have been ridiculed for making such a big deal over the purity and clarity of the cross. But my friend's words revealed to me just how big, and just how divisive, the cross can be.

The Bible says we are saved by grace through faith in Jesus Christ. By faith I had embraced the cross of Jesus, but because I didn't embrace my friend's "sinner's prayer," he was no longer embracing me.

Like many, my friend believed prayer was necessary for salvation. So, even though the Scriptures said otherwise, he doubted I was saved. He asked me, "If you didn't pray, then how do you know you're saved?"

I didn't want to argue with my missionary friend; I wanted to help him. So, directing him back to the word of God, I answered, "The Bible says, 'Believe on the Lord Jesus Christ, and you shall be saved'. Brother Don, I believe on the Lord Jesus Christ. What do *you* say? Am I saved?"

My question put Brother Don in a hard position. For, if he said I was not saved, he would be contradicting the apostle Paul (Acts 16:31). But, if he agreed with Paul, he'd be contradicting himself and would have to acknowledge his wrong.

"Well, if you believe on Jesus, I guess you are saved. But, when I go to Mexico [as a missionary], I want to hear them pray. That way I will *know* they are saved," he said in an exasperated tone.

8 SO CLOSE, YET SO FAR AWAY

In both the Old and New Testaments, people were saved only one way: by faith. *Even as Abraham believed God, and it was accounted to him for righteousness* (Galatians 3:6).

Why, then, were my pastor and missionary friend so offended by my faith in Jesus? How could they reject a simple and sincere faith in the gospel of Jesus Christ? Jesus said, *"He that believes on him is not condemned . . ."* (John 3:18). Don't Baptists believe salvation is by faith, like Jesus said?

The answer is yes. The Bible teaches that salvation is by grace through faith in Jesus, and Baptists (like my former pastor and missionary friend) do believe this doctrine as well. So, if we all believed salvation was by faith, why was my faith in Christ creating this conflict?

The conflict arose because my church had mistakenly substituted a surrendered life and heartfelt prayer for faith in Jesus Christ. Like many churches, they had essentially redefined the meaning of faith. This is a favorite tactic of the Devil, because it allows people to use Bible words without knowing Bible truths.

I was telling people to trust in the salvation Jesus accomplished on the cross. They were telling people to trust God to save them, when they prayed and surrendered their lives to Him. And, though I was not trying to be controversial, my message of salvation by faith in Jesus was conflicting with their message of prayer and surrender.

But if people could be saved by praying and surrendering, then

Jesus would have never had to die on the cross. The Bible makes it very clear that there is no salvation without the cross of Jesus Christ. It says *"the preaching of the cross"* is the power of God unto salvation (1 Corinthians 1:18).

Make no mistake: you can pray a sincere prayer to God and surrender your whole life to Him and still miss the cross. The Pharisees made long prayers to God, but they didn't trust in Jesus. As a result, the Pharisees did not go to heaven.

Before his conversion to Christ, the apostle Paul (a Pharisee) had fully surrendered his life to God. He was willing to do whatever God told Him to do. Nevertheless, he was not saved, until he embraced the cross of Jesus. And, because he did embrace the cross, Paul went to heaven. In the end, despite all his religious accomplishments, Paul summed up his faith like this in Galatians 6:14: *"But God forbid that I should boast, except in the cross of our Lord Jesus Christ . . ."*

In his sermon, "Salvation at the Cross", Spurgeon said, "Any faith that rests short of the cross is a faith that will land you short of Heaven." This is why the Devil is perfectly happy with any religious thing you do, as long as you do not put your trust in the Savior who bled and died in your place. The Devil wants you to put your faith in anything, as long as you never put your faith where God put your sin—in the Savior who was crucified for you.

Lest the reader think I am splitting hairs, I will share an encounter I had with a certain church member one night. Shortly after I was saved, I shared my testimony with the church. At the close of service, a church member confronted me in the fellowship hall, taking issue with something I said.

"You said even if a person prays, if that person does not put his faith in what Jesus did on the cross, then that person is not saved."

"That's correct. A person must put his faith in Jesus to be saved. That's what the Bible says," I affirmed.

He responded, "Let me give you my testimony: When I was a young man, I was working in a rice field one day, when I heard the audible voice of God with my own ears. And, when I heard God's voice, I fell down on my knees and cried out to Him to save me."

I must admit, being in a rice field and hearing God's voice with your own ears is quite a dramatic testimony. But where was Jesus in that drama? Though his story was dramatic, it was missing the gospel. I looked him in the eyes and said, "Brother Al, if you didn't put your faith in Jesus, then you were not saved."

One would think this man would have immediately responded, "Oh yes! Of course I placed my faith in Jesus that day!" But, instead, he argued, "But, I fell on my knees in the mud!" Reader, do you see the difference? Atonement for sin is not accomplished by falling on our knees in the mud; it is accomplished by Jesus giving His life for us on a cross. To trust in the former is to perish in your sins; to trust in the latter is to *"not perish, but have everlasting life"* (John 3:16).

When Jesus said, in John 6:53, *"Except you eat the flesh of the Son of man, and drink his blood, you have no life in you."* He made it very clear that eternal life is not found at the altar, nor beside your bed, nor in a rice field, but only at the cross where He would shed His blood and die for our sins. Of course, we can trust in the crucified Savior anywhere, including a rice field, but we dare not go to any place without trusting in the one who took our place.

We have been given a clear and powerful message of salvation in the Bible. But when that message is not communicated clearly in the pulpit, it can't be comprehended clearly in the pew. Those who do not understand salvation will be more prone to doubt it. Or, worse, as this man, they will vainly trust in something else.

For this reason, some people attend church their entire lives and never have the full assurance that they are saved. Some stop attending church, because the fiery "salvation" sermons they hear give them agony, but they do not give them answers. Some occupy leadership positions in the church, and they are too embarrassed to ask for help. As leaders, they not only wrestle with doubts about their salvation, but they wrestle with the burden of trying to help others while knowing they can't even help themselves.

Having a "gospel" that's so close, yet so far away from the cross, leaves people in confusion and doubt. There are people today, who are longing to know that their sins are forgiven and that heaven is their home. Are you one of these people? If you are, take heart: this book was written for you.

9 A PURPOSE FOR THE PAIN

I couldn't understand why Christianity had to be so difficult for me. Why did God make me suffer that long ordeal of doubt, fear, and confusion? Why did I have to lose my beloved church family? I didn't know the answers to these things, but there were some things I did know as a result of this painful experience.

I knew the fear of going to hell was one of the most dreadful things a person could endure. And I knew that, wherever the gospel was perverted, there would be other people experiencing this fear and longing for peace. So, during my time of doubt, I determined that if God ever delivered me from the confusion I was in, I would do what I could to help others who were in that same condition.

After suffering the embarrassment of being the preacher "who got saved," the last thing I wanted to do was preach again. But God planned otherwise. Unbeknownst to me, God was going to use the things I had suffered to help reach others with the gospel message. Like a wise blacksmith, God was using the confusion, pain, and fear I had experienced to bring me to a red-hot heat that He might, by the continual pounding of my adversity, forge sound doctrine in my heart and fashion me into the servant He had foreordained me to be.

I had gone through a very difficult struggle. But, God was using that struggle to make me painfully aware of the errors of evangelism, of the truth of the gospel, and of the fiery arrows Satan shoots at men when they are confused and searching for answers. Though I desired to stay behind the scenes, God wanted me to give others the wonderful truths He had so graciously given to me. So, after I was asked to leave my church, God led me to a different Baptist church—one where the gospel was clearly preached and where I could rest, heal, and grow in my new faith in Christ.

So, along with my new faith, I found a new burden—a burden to tell others about the life-giving truth of Jesus and the power of His cross. Of course, the Devil doesn't give up lost territory easily. I still had to work through some issues with doctrine and occasional doubt. But God was faithful. In time, He helped me overcome these things, and He caused me to grow in grace and in the knowledge of my Lord and Savior Jesus Christ.

As I grew, God put a hunger in my heart to learn His Word and to share it with others. To satisfy this hunger, He opened doors for me to preach the gospel at local correctional facilities. And, within a few years, I had finished seminary, and I was pastoring my first church.

My time in the pastorate was rewarding, but my heart remained heavy for people who doubted their salvation. I enjoyed teaching the people in my church, but I wanted to somehow reach the people beyond my church who were struggling with doubt. I knew they were out there; I knew people were struggling, but I didn't know how to find them.

How can I reach these people? Should I use a billboard? Should I start a radio program?

I wasn't sure what to do, so I just kept doing what I was doing: pastoring my church, while carrying this awkward burden on my heart. My burden remained until 2006, when I suddenly experienced vocal trouble and was unable to continue pastoring. A preacher's voice is like a pianist's hands, and I couldn't understand why God took my voice away. I could still talk, but my voice was too weak to handle the demands of pastoral teaching.

Frustrated and confused, I stepped down from the pastorate, and I waited on God to show me what to do. I was afraid God had rejected my ministry. I wondered if I had done something wrong. But, as I sought God's will for my life, I suddenly realized that this break from the ministry would give me an opportunity to reach people who were struggling with doubt.

No longer burdened with the demands of pastoring a church,

God laid it on my heart to create a website that would focus on helping people who doubted their salvation. I figured I could rest my voice enough to record one message. And, then, little by little, I could add new messages until there were enough to sufficiently explain the gospel and cover some of the issues I had struggled with. So, in 2007, with the backing of my church, we launched the website and prayed God would lead the people to it who needed help.

God answered our prayers. Shortly after launching the website, people began visiting the site and listening to the messages. And, within a few years, I had received emails and phone calls from people all over the United States, Canada, and from as far away as South Africa, who were seeking assurance of their salvation.

I was so thankful to finally have a venue to reach these people. Sadly, however, ministering to these people caused me to realize that our vast network of missionaries, seminaries, and itinerant preachers had managed to spread the same unbiblical teachings and clichés that had confused me to people all over the world. And the problem was even deeper than this. For, not only did I have regular church members contacting me about their salvation, but I had pastors, church workers, and Bible college students, reaching out to me for help as well.

All of these dear people had one thing in common: they all had some misconception of the gospel, and they all doubted their salvation because of it. And this was not limited to a single denomination. People from many different denominations, and with a wide range of religious backgrounds and experiences, were writing in for help. But, regardless of their different backgrounds, they all had the same basic problem and the same burning desire to know they were saved.

So, with each person I spoke to, I was determined to know nothing among them, *"except Jesus Christ, and him crucified."* And I am a witness today that the gospel is still the power of God unto salvation unto all who believe. For, I have seen God save and comfort many of these people through a simple message of what Christ has done for them and their faith in that message.

In 2 Corinthians 1:6, the apostle Paul said, if *"we be afflicted, it is for your consolation and salvation..."* I know now that there was a purpose for my pain. God allowed me to be *afflicted* so that others could be *saved* and *comforted*. He allowed me to fall into the dark ditch of doubt, so I could take the gracious ladder He gave me, by which I climbed out, and lower that ladder down to you.

Sometimes this ladder is hard to see and climb, even when it is right in front of you. Our enemy, the Devil, has many tricks up his sleeve to discourage you from using the gospel ladder and climbing out of the ditch. He will assault your heart with despair and confusion, making even the simple things seem complicated. Have you not found it so?

Take courage beloved, for Jesus' cross has defeated the Devil. His cross reaches all the way down into the deepest ditch, and you (by God's grace) can surely take hold of it and climb out. In the remaining chapters of this book, we will examine things that may be hindering your faith—those obstacles that commonly stand in the way of people being saved or that steal away the assurance they desire. And, by shining the light of God's Word upon them, I pray you will see the ladder, climb out of the ditch, and come to a sure and saving knowledge of Jesus Christ.

10 I DON'T KNOW IF I'M SAVED OR LOST

As I stated in the previous chapter, I have spoken to many people who've doubted their salvation, and they all shared one thing in common: they all had some misunderstanding of the gospel. I cannot emphasize this to you enough. If you doubt your salvation, it is because you have a fundamental misunderstanding of how salvation works. There is some flaw in your theology, some bad doctrinal baggage you are carrying around, or some small piece of the gospel puzzle you're missing.

This does not necessarily mean you are lost. I don't believe everyone I've spoken to has been lost. I'm sure many were, but I believe many were also true believers who (at the time) simply had some flaw in their belief system—some distraction that was taking their eyes off Jesus and His cross.

Consider the Olympic runner. He is well-trained, and he has excellent genetics. But if a small stone finds its way into the runner's shoe, his race will be greatly hindered. The best he can do is hobble down the track. But once the stone is removed, he can run the race as he intended.

Like a stone in your shoe, if you have a flaw in your belief system, your race will be greatly hindered. But when the doctrinal error is removed, you will be able to run the race as God intended. And if it is *not* removed, then you will continue to hobble down the track in pain, or you will sit on the sideline in despair.

Just as Peter sank into the sea when he took his eyes off Jesus (Matthew 14:30), so Christians can take their eyes off Jesus and sink into doubt. A Christian may fall into sin, for example, and begin doubting her faith and her love for God. Or a false teacher may tell her she must speak in tongues to be saved, and she could begin doubting her experience. Or, again, if she does not experience a sense of peace one day, she could begin focusing on the way she feels, instead of focusing on Jesus.

Unfortunately, these type "stones" are commonly found in Christian shoes. The Apostles had to help Christians remove these stones in their day, and Christians in our day are no different. The Devil loves to harass our minds. He will cause us to question the sincerity of our repentance, the integrity of our faith, and the genuineness of our experience and love for Christ. And, if we get our eyes off Jesus, and focus on these things, this will cause us to sink into doubt.

When our eyes should be on Jesus, they will instead be on our *works*, our *prayers*, our *faith*, our *repentance*, or on our *love* and *endurance* for God. If this happens to you, after you have trusted in the sacrifice of Christ, this does not mean you are *lost*; it means (for the time) you are *distracted*. And you'll have to correct this, by putting your eyes back on the salvation Jesus accomplished for you, before you can experience assurance again.

Here is the great take away from all this. For a *lost* person to be saved, that person must understand the gospel and rest his or her faith in Jesus alone. Likewise, for a *saved* person to regain assurance of salvation, that person must understand the gospel and (by renewing the mind) rest his or her faith in Jesus alone.

So, whether you are saved or lost, if you doubt your salvation, the solution to your problem is the same. To have a bold, confident assurance of your salvation, you must have:

1) A clear understanding of the gospel and
2) A complete reliance on the gospel you understand.

So, you don't have to waste your time trying to figure out if you are saved or lost. Countless hours have been spent by people trying to figure out if they were saved at some time in the past. But, whether you are lost or saved, you simply need to have a clear understanding of the gospel and rely on that gospel for your salvation. If you will keep this in mind, this will make things very simple for you, and hopefully, it will give you a speedy end to your struggle. The purpose of the next chapter, therefore, will be to help you gain a clear understanding of the gospel.

11 UNDERSTANDING THE GOSPEL

The word "sin" means to *come short* [of God's perfect standard]. When God created us, we were supposed to be the glory of God in heaven here on earth. The Bible says man... *"is the image and glory of God"* (1 Corinthians 11:7). But, because we have all disobeyed God, we have all sinned (come short) of the divine glory we were supposed to be. Romans 3:23 says, *"all have sinned, and come short of the glory of God..."*

To understand the gospel, you must understand that God is a perfect and holy God. And, to be accepted by a perfect and holy God, you must be a perfect and holy person.

Assume for a moment that you could live a sin-free life ninety percent of the time. I don't believe anybody can actually achieve 90 percent obedience (I know I couldn't), but let's suppose *you* could. If God were to accept you being only ninety percent good, then He would have to lower His standard ten percent, to accept you at ninety.

Of course, God would never lower His standard. For, if He lowered His standard down to yours, not only would you still be unholy, but then He would be unholy, too. So, the question we have to ask ourselves is this: How can a perfect and holy God accept imperfect and unholy people—people who "come short" of His perfect standard without lowering His standard in the least degree?

Only the gospel of Jesus Christ can solve this dilemma. Let me explain.

When the first man, Adam, was in the garden of Eden, he represented the entire human race. Therefore, when Adam disobeyed God, he caused the whole human race (you and me) to become sinners. Romans 5:19 says, *"by one man's disobedience many were made sinners . . ."*

Since we became sinners on account of Adam, Jesus came to undo what Adam did. Understand, then, when Jesus was born, He was not just the babe in a manger; He was the *second* Adam.

1 Corinthians 15:45-47 says, *"And so it is written, The first man Adam was made a living soul; the last Adam was made a quickening spirit . . . The first man is of the earth, earthy: the second man is the Lord from heaven."*

As the second Adam, Jesus would be tempted, just like the first Adam, but (unlike the first Adam) Jesus would never sin. Jesus would perfectly obey God's Word! So, by *doing* what the first Adam *didn't* do, Jesus would *undo* what the first Adam did.

This is why Jesus, after He was baptized by John the Baptist, immediately went into the wilderness to be tempted of the Devil, as mentioned in Matthew 4:1, *"Then was Jesus led up of the Spirit into the wilderness to be tempted of the devil."*

As Adam was tempted in the *garden*, so Jesus would be tempted in the *desert*. But, unlike the first Adam, when Jesus was tempted, He never sinned. Jesus resisted Satan's temptation, and, no matter how difficult those temptations became in His life, He never disobeyed His heavenly Father. Because Jesus loved you, He did everything right. Throughout Jesus' entire life, He fully obeyed God 100 percent of the time. He did not come short. Hebrews 4:15 says Jesus *"was in all points tempted like as we are, yet without sin."* If you want to know that heaven is your home, this book was written for you.

And the Bible says Jesus continued His perfect obedience all the way to the cross, where He died for our sins, as mentioned in Philippians 2:8: *"And being found in fashion as a man, he humbled himself, and became obedient unto death, even the death of the cross."*

Here is the most wonderful part of all: On the cross, Jesus took credit for how YOU lived, so you could get credit for how HE lived. 2 Corinthians 5:21 says God *"made him to be sin for us, who knew no sin; that we might be made the righteousness of God in him."*

When Jesus was on the cross, He was tried, sentenced, and condemned for your *sinful* life, so you could be tried, acquitted, and accepted by His *sinless* life!

```
      ✝  Righteousness (Innocence) →
         ← Sin (Guilt)              🚶
```

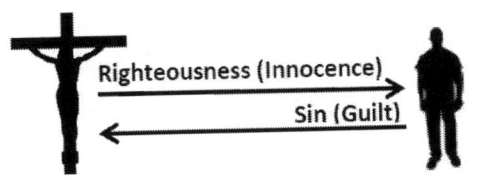

Imagine that you are in a court of law. In this court, God (the Judge) is seated at the Judge's bench, and you (the person being judged) are seated at the defendant's table. In front of you is a book. It is the book of your life. The first page of the book documents your birth, and the last page documents your death. And, all the pages in between contain everything you ever said, everything you ever thought, and everything you ever did—your entire life. In a moment, God is going to call you to the bench, and you will hand Him your book, and He will judge you according to all your deeds written therein.

If God were to open this book of your life and judge you according to everything you've done, would He find that you perfectly obeyed His Word throughout your entire life? Or, would He find that you sinned, and came short of His perfect standard? If you are honest, you will admit you've come short. Romans 3:23 makes it clear: *"For all have sinned, and come short . . ."*

Since you are a sinner, if God judges you according to the book of your life, you will be found to have come short of His perfect standard, and you will be rejected and condemned.

But imagine now that there is *another* book at the defendant's table. It is the book of Jesus' life. The first page of the book tells of Jesus' virgin birth, and the last page declares His sacrificial death. And all the pages in between contain everything Jesus ever said, everything Jesus ever thought, and everything Jesus ever did—His entire life. Now, what if, before God calls you to the bench to be judged, He makes you a very gracious offer: Instead of judging you according to the book of *your* life, God says you can toss your book in the shredder and hand Him the book of Jesus' life instead. Surely, if God judged you according to how *Jesus* lived, He would find no fault in you.

Reader, if God gave you that option, would you take it? Would you allow God to judge you, not on the basis of how you lived, but on the basis of how Jesus lived and died in your place? If you answer yes, I have good news for you: God has made you this offer.

The gospel is the good news that God has made a way for you to be accepted by Him on the merit of another person: Jesus Christ. Romans 5:19 says, *"For as by one man's [Adam's] disobedience many were made sinners, so by the obedience of one [Jesus] shall many be made righteous."*

Every time the gospel is preached, God is reaching out to condemned sinners, offering them an opportunity to no longer be condemned, on account of how they've lived, but to be declared perfect (justified) on account of how Jesus lived and died in their place. Understand, therefore, that Jesus Christ lived and died as your substitute. When Jesus obeyed God, it was (by His representation) you who obeyed God, for Jesus lived in your place. And when Jesus died on the cross, it was you who died on the cross, for Jesus died in your place. *"Christ died for the ungodly"* (Romans 5:6).

Two thousand years ago, you were tried, sentenced, and condemned for all your sins on the cross. Therefore, if you will accept God's offer, you need not fear being condemned twice for the same crimes. God will not require the penalty to be paid by Jesus, and then require it again from you. That would be double jeopardy. And that is why Jesus said, *"He that believes on him is not condemned . . ."* (John 3:18).

The cross, therefore, is like a giant shredder, where the record of your guilty life was forever put away. The gospel has lovingly placed the sinless life of Jesus on the defendant's table, and, if you will have it, the Judge is ready to accept His book instead of yours.

Faith, then, is a decision you make to accept this gracious offer from God. Faith is when you allow God to shred the book of your life at the cross, and to judge you instead according to the life and death of His only begotten Son. Reader, will you accept God's offer? Will you allow Him to judge you, not on the basis of how you have lived, but on the basis of how Jesus lived and died in your place?

If you will accept God's offer, if you will stake your soul's eternity upon the merit of Jesus Christ, you will most surely be saved, for that is why Jesus came. 1 Timothy 1:15 says, *"This is a faithful saying, and worthy of all acceptation, that Christ Jesus came into the world to save sinners . . ."* So, if you will accept Jesus, then, God will accept you. What is your decision?

HOW SHALL GOD JUDGE YOU?

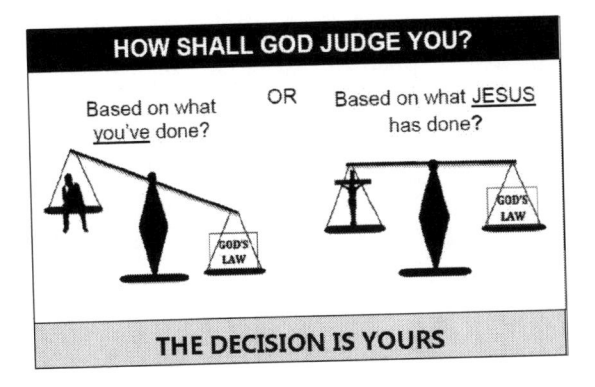

Based on what you've done?   OR   Based on what JESUS has done?

THE DECISION IS YOURS

12 GETTING BACK TO THE BIBLE

The Word of God is absolutely essential to understanding the gospel and knowing we are saved. There is simply no other resource that can give us eternal life, and the assurance that we have it, than God's Holy Word. Our faith, therefore, must be based on a clear understanding of the gospel, as it is presented to us in the Bible (1 Corinthians 1:21-23).

Unfortunately, however, a person would be hard-pressed to find a clear presentation of the gospel in many pulpits today. Oddly enough, my former pastor did not believe a clear presentation of the gospel was necessary for salvation. He told me, "I don't believe we should worry about whether or not we preach the gospel correctly, because I believe the Holy Spirit is powerful enough to overcome anything we tell someone that may be incorrect, and He can save them in spite of it." To this day, I am still amazed by his statement.

Let me be clear, salvation is of the Lord. Only God can open the eyes of the lost. The clearest presentation of the gospel cannot save a single soul, unless the Spirit of God opens that person's heart and eyes to understand it and receive it. Nevertheless, when churches fail to teach the gospel clearly, they are most certainly to blame when their members don't understand it. God has chosen the preaching of the cross to save them that believe, and the Apostle Paul said "though we, or an angel from heaven, preach any other gospel unto you than that which we have preached unto you, let him be accursed" (Galatians 1:8).

So, if the gospel is presented to us clearly in the Bible, then why is it sometimes not presented clearly in the church? Well, remember, the corruption of the gospel message is nothing new. The apostles were fighting it back in their day, and we will continue fighting it in ours. The difference for us today is *how* it is being corrupted. The corruption today is so subtle that a preacher can actually appear to be proclaiming the gospel, and yet (amazingly) never mention the gospel at all.

In 1998, I received a promotion at work and was transferred to another town. Of course, moving to a new town meant I had to find a new church. Naturally, I wanted to make sure my new pastor was solid on the gospel.

To accomplish this, I sat down with a prospective pastor one day, and I told him, "I want you to pretend like I am lost, and lead me to Christ." Consenting to my request, the pastor:

1. Told me I was a sinner and couldn't save myself.
2. Told me salvation was by grace through faith alone and not of my good works.
3. And, then, he concluded by telling me I needed to call upon the Lord and ask Him to save me.

Having finished the above presentation, the pastor asked me, "Well, how did I do?"

No doubt, the vast majority of Christians would have found nothing wrong with the pastor's "gospel" presentation. After all, it sounds so orthodox. But the pastor was surprised by my response.

"You left one thing out sir."

Puzzled, the pastor asked me, "What did I leave out?"

"The cross. You never told me that Jesus died for me on the cross."

For that matter, the pastor also never told me that Jesus was buried, or that He rose again from the dead. Amazingly, in the pastor's "gospel" presentation, the gospel was never mentioned. And only God knows how many people that pastor has led in an empty exercise of praying for "salvation," without ever telling them about the salvation Jesus accomplished for them through His death, burial, and resurrection in their place.

It is meaningless to tell people salvation is "by faith" if we don't tell them what their faith is supposed to be in. Faith in a bloodless offering didn't help Cain, and faith in a bloodless prayer won't help me and you.

Jesus died as a substitute for us on the cross, but nothing can be a substitute for Jesus. Living a good life, getting baptized, taking the mass, "giving your heart to Jesus," having a "personal relationship" with Jesus, asking Jesus "into your heart," or asking God to save you—these things may sound warm and fuzzy, but apart from trusting in Jesus' sacrifice on the cross (faith in Christ), there is no forgiveness of sins. God said in Leviticus 17:11, *"it is the blood that makes an atonement for the soul."* So, don't place your faith in the above things and fall short of placing it in Jesus, for only Jesus shed His blood and died to make an atonement (to cover your sin with His sacrifice) for your soul.

The success of any society hinges on its citizens' ability to assimilate and operate under a common set of rules. The rules we have been given to operate under are God's words. But, when a society rejects God, people generally accept the rules of the majority and follow the crowd.

This is why our clothing, hairstyles, and trends continually go in and out of fashion, as people see and follow the actions of others. This is why people can see somebody doing something on television, and then, no matter how ridiculous it is, they will start doing it, too. It's strange, but this is how humans behave. And, this is why we need God's unchanging Word.

The gospel is corrupted in the church when preachers mimic the words and actions of men without first scrutinizing them with the words of God. All too often, preachers adopt poor gospel presentations simply because they hear other preachers using them. Once again, people tend to follow other people.

Failing to stick with God's Word, trend-setting preachers will sometimes deviate from the Bible, preaching empty "salvation" messages that encourage their hearers to perform some outward physical action (pray, come forward, turn their lives over to God, etc.), rather than encouraging them to believe in the salvation Jesus accomplished. Other preachers will then follow their lead, echoing what they've seen and heard the popular preacher do and say, giving little regard for its biblical basis.

One such trend-setting preacher is the late Dr. Jack Hyles, former pastor of First Baptist Church in Hammond, Indiana. Pastor Hyles had 20,000 people attend his church each week, and his teachings on "soul winning" still influence how people share the gospel today. Although Pastor Hyles did preach the gospel, some of his "soul winning" tactics were not based on God's word.

Faith (believing) is an *inward spiritual* response to the gospel message. Jesus promised in John 3:15 that *"whosoever believes in Him should not perish, but have everlasting life."* But, with no Biblical authority for doing so, Pastor Hyles encouraged people to perform *outward physical* responses to his gospel message. And the physical actions he imposed often distracted them from the gospel message.

For example, Pastor Hyles was a strong believer in getting people to pray a "sinner's prayer" for salvation. Additionally, after they prayed the "sinner's prayer," Pastor Hyles would also ask them to take him by the hand, as a way of symbolizing them taking Jesus by the hand as their Savior. Pastor Hyles' book, "Let's Go Soul Winning", was his step-by-step guide to leading someone to Christ. Listen to the following excerpt from that book:

> "He has just prayed and asked the Lord to save him. 'Now Mr. Doe, while our heads are bowed, if Jesus Christ came in the room, He would extend His hand, no doubt, and ask you to take His hand if you would receive Him. Mr. Doe, if you will make this day the day of your salvation and this moment receive Christ as your Saviour, just like my hand were His hand, would you put your hand in mine?' Now, he takes your hand."

By using these tactics, I'm sure Pastor Hyles got a lot of people to recite that prayer and give him their hands. But tactics like this are nothing more than human manipulation. The Holy Spirit saves people through the preaching of the gospel and faith in Jesus Christ, not through praying a prayer and taking the preacher's hand.

Pastor Hyles' style of "sinner's prayer" evangelism was adopted by many churches, and I myself became a victim of it. As a lost teenager, I gathered with others at my church every Tuesday evening to go "soul winning". We would go door to door throughout the neighborhoods, asking everyone we met if they were saved, and leading them in a "sinner's prayer" if they were not. We were so well trained that I could get someone to recite the "sinner's prayer" with me within five minutes of me knocking on their door. Like a good vacuum cleaner salesman, I had the sales pitch down, and I led many people in those prayers.

In addition to going door to door, we ran a bus route to get children into church. Perhaps no demographic group yielded more professed "salvations" than the children. From Sunday morning children's church, to summer youth camps, the young people were a fruitful field who were ripe for our evangelistic picking.

I can still see all those little hands going up in children's church. The teacher would tell the children about a terrible place called hell and about a wonderful place called heaven. Then, the teacher would ask the children, "How many of you want to go to hell?"

Naturally, no child dared raise his or her hand. After all, nobody wants to burn forever. So, the teacher would ask, "Who wants to go to heaven?" and numerous hands would be raised, providing the teacher an opportunity to lead them in a "sinner's prayer".

Do you see the tragedy in all of this? I was raised in church. I was trained to "win souls" for Christ. I volunteered in the children's church services. And I went to youth camp. But, somehow, in all those ministries, the gospel was lost, and so was I.

I'm not saying everyone in that church was lost. I know there were some who truly trusted in Jesus. But I also know the evangelistic tactics that we thought were reaching the lost were actually giving many a false assurance of salvation and making the gospel more difficult for them to understand.

We will learn more about the "sinner's prayer" in the next chapter. But, for now, I want you to understand that you must resist the inventions of men and stick with the Word of God. When it comes to your salvation, the only thing *you* have to do is believe in what *Jesus* has already done.

Another trend setter was an 1800s revival preacher named Charles Finney. Mr. Finney's view on salvation was so far off that it would not be accepted by most pastors today. However, in spite of Mr. Finney's erroneous view of the gospel, he still has an extraordinary influence on our pastors today. Why? Because Mr. Finney is the one who popularized the "altar call."

Although the "altar call" (or having the sinner come forward) is commonly practiced in our American churches, and was once a hallmark in Billy Graham's crusades, it was once unheard of by the church. Though the "altar call" is nowhere in the Bible, Christians have now come to accept it as standard biblical practice. In fact, I have had people refuse to join my church simply because I do not give an "altar call" at the end of my sermon.

One of the most powerful books in the New Testament is the

book of Hebrews. The book of Hebrews was trying to convince the Hebrew people to no longer trust in the animal sacrifices but to put their faith in the sacrifice of Jesus Christ. The Holy Spirit, therefore, has called for us to leave those Old Testament altars behind. And I believe the New Testament church made a great mistake when she (without Biblical authority) created new altars to take their place.

Those Old Testament altars were replaced by the cross of Jesus Christ. The cross is where God was satisfied. The cross is where our debt was paid. The cross is where peace with God was forever made by the blood Jesus shed for us. The cross is the only place where we (in Christ) can truly die to sin and self, and not some bloodless "altar" we invented at the front of our churches.

Like praying the sinner's prayer and taking the preacher by the hand, the altar call promotes an outward physical response to the gospel message. It calls for people to *come forward* and *pray*, but the gospel seeks an inward spiritual response. It calls for us to believe its message and trust in Jesus' salvation. Because our fallen nature is so prone to idolatry, we shouldn't add anything to our gospel presentation that has the potential to distract, confuse, or compete with the simple message of a Savior who was crucified for sinners.

Preachers have long encouraged people to come down to an "old-fashioned altar." But if we truly want an old-fashioned religion, then we don't need to get people to the altar; we need to get them to Jesus, and we need to get them back to the Word of God. This is what I pray God will accomplish with this book.

13 THE SINNER'S PRAYER

I believe the "sinner's prayer" has created more confusion, generated more false professions, and has done more to launch us toward the great apostasy than any other error that has crept into the modern church. Having gained widespread acceptance in the 20th Century, partly due to its use by TV and radio evangelists, the "sinner's prayer" has since become a staple for modern evangelism and an icon for the dumbing down of the American church.

With so many preachers offering their listeners a "sinner's prayer" to say at the end of their sermons, one would expect the Bible to be full of scriptures about this special "prayer" for salvation. But, the truth is, the Bible verses used by "sinner's prayer" evangelists are very few, and they are very misunderstood.

Although Romans 10:9-13 doesn't teach a "sinner's prayer," many evangelists quote this passage as their premier authority for using it. Since I have dedicated two chapters of this book to explaining Romans 10:9-13 (Chapters 14 and 15), I will reserve my comments on that passage for those chapters. So, setting aside the book of Romans for now, let's talk about Revelation 3:20, for it is the second verse that's most quoted by "sinner's prayer" evangelists.

We have heard it all our lives. It's warm; it's fuzzy; and it sounds so good to our emotional ears. The pastor stands a young child before the congregation and announces to the church that little Susan has just "asked Jesus to come into her heart!"

Ambitious church workers have long encouraged young people to "ask Jesus to come into their hearts" (to be saved), and they have used Revelation 3:20 as their basis for doing so. But, is this what the Bible really teaches? In Revelation 3:20, Jesus told the Church of Laodicea, *"Behold, I stand at the door, and knock: if any man hear my voice, and open the door, I will come in to him, and will sup with him, and he with me."*

Although the human heart is never mentioned in the above passage, evangelists have taken this one Bible verse and promised eternal life to untold thousands if they would only "open the door of their heart" and ask Jesus to come in. But this is not what the verse promises. Let's take a closer look at what Jesus said.

In this verse, Jesus neither mentions *salvation* nor the *heart*. Furthermore, He never said He would come "into" anybody. There is a big difference between the words "in to" and the word "into." Jesus said, *"I will come in to him . . ."* Jesus did not say, "I will come *into* him . . ."

In other words, Jesus was not saying He was going to come into (inside) anybody. He said He was going to *"come in to"* the person who opened the door. That is, He would come in to wherever they were.

Like the vacated temple in the book of Ezekiel, it appears that the Laodicean church had figuratively lost the presence of Christ. And, in Revelation 3:20, Jesus told the church that if any man would open the door and let Him in, then He would come in and sup or eat with that person. The emphasis, therefore, is on the Lord Jesus' presence and fellowship with His people.

In fact, in Revelation 3:20, there is nothing directly stated about forgiveness, the new birth, or salvation. So, if we're not careful, we can read too much into this passage and get the mechanics of the gospel completely backward. Salvation does not come by Jesus entering through the door of sinners; salvation comes by sinners entering through the door of Jesus. Jesus said in John 10:9, *"I am the door: by me if any man enter in, he shall be saved . . ."*

Nevertheless, because Jesus said He stood at the "door" and knocked, many preachers teach that Jesus is now knocking at the "door" of sinners' hearts and that (to be saved) those sinners must "open the door of their hearts" and let Jesus come in. And this can cause would-be Christians to trust in whatever they imagine Jesus will do when He comes "into their hearts," instead of trusting in what they know Jesus did when He died on the cross for their sins. In Acts 16:30-31, a lost jail keeper asked Paul and Silas this question, *"Sirs, what must I do to be saved?"* And Paul and Silas gave them a clear and simple answer to that question, when they said, *"Believe on the Lord Jesus Christ, and you shall be saved . . ."*

Paul and Silas made no mention of a prayer. But, because the "sinner's prayer" has become so widely accepted, it's sometimes difficult for Christians to comprehend how people can be saved without it. People frequently ask me, "But, if you don't tell people to pray (for salvation), what *do* you tell them to do?"

The apostle Paul told the jailer to believe on Jesus to be saved. This is also what Jesus said we must do. But, sadly, the biblical concept of believing in Jesus for salvation has become so foreign to the church that many churches no longer know how.

Do you remember in the last chapter when I said we must get back to the Bible? May I humbly ask you, dear reader? Can you show me one instance in the Bible where Jesus, or one of His apostles, ever led someone in a "sinner's prayer"? I'm not asking you if you've ever read a scripture that makes you think a "sinner's prayer" might exist. I'm asking you if you have a single Bible example where our Lord, or one of His apostles (or anyone for that matter), ever led someone in a prayer for salvation.

And, if Jesus and the apostles did not do this in their day, shouldn't we ask ourselves why we do it today? And must we not conclude that *our* evangelism differs from *their* evangelism? Upon what Scriptural authority, then, do we deviate from their example? Not only is the "sinner's prayer" absent from Scripture, I have personally never seen a "sinner's prayer" in a sermon preached prior to the 20th Century.

Let's talk about the difference of the sinner's prayer; that is, how does salvation through *prayer* differ from salvation through *faith*? Ephesians 2:8 says, *"For by grace are you saved through faith . . ."* Grace is God's gift of salvation through Christ's death on the cross. Faith is our belief (trust) in that grace.

God the Father, therefore, has made Jesus' death on the cross the object of our faith. When Jesus spoke to Nicodemus about his salvation, He told him in John 3:14-15, *"And as Moses lifted up the serpent in the wilderness, even so must the Son of man be lifted up* [on the cross]*: That whosoever believes* [has faith] *in him should not perish, but have eternal life."*

When Jesus mentioned Moses lifting up the serpent, He was referring to an event in Numbers 21 where God punished Israel's rebellion with a plague of fiery (venomous) snakes. After many of the Israelites died from snake bites, the people finally repented and asked Moses to pray that God would take away the snakes. What's fascinating is how God responded to Moses' prayer.

In Numbers 21:8, we are told, *"And the Lord said unto Moses, Make you a fiery serpent, and set it upon a pole: and it shall come to pass, that every one that is bitten, when he looks upon it, shall live."*

The scripture then goes on to say in verse 9, *"And Moses made a serpent of brass, and put it upon a pole, and it came to pass, that if a serpent had bitten any man, when he beheld the serpent of brass, he lived."*

Jesus, therefore, explained to Nicodemus that, just as Moses lifted up the serpent of brass on a pole, and all who looked to it were saved, *in the same way,* He (Jesus) would be lifted up on a cross, and everyone who believes in Him on that cross would not perish but have eternal life.

What did those people see when they beheld the serpent of brass on the pole? They saw the very thing that was causing them to die (a serpent). And that serpent was made of brass—the same material the brazen altar was made of—the altar where *sacrifice* was made for their sins.

Likewise, when we look to Jesus on the cross, we see the very thing that's causing us to die (sin). And, like the brass of the serpent, we see Jesus offered as a sacrifice for that sin. We behold it; we believe it, and we are saved!

Notice that God did not tell the people in the wilderness to pray to the brazen serpent and ask it to come into their hearts. Likewise, we are not told to pray to Jesus and ask Him to come into our hearts. In the wilderness, there was no promise of being saved from the *serpents* made to anyone but to those who looked away from themselves and set their eyes upon the serpent that was lifted up for them. Accordingly, there is no promise of being saved from *sin* made to anyone but to those who look away from themselves and set their eyes upon the Savior who was lifted up for them.

You must understand that the Devil wants you to beg God over and over again to save you. But, God doesn't want you to beg in misery; God wants you to rest in peace. He wants you to put your eyes of faith on the Savior, who was lifted up for you, and rest in the salvation He accomplished. Reader, will you do that?

Perhaps you are thinking, *"But some people may have prayed when they looked upon the serpent!"* Well, I suppose some people did pray that day. But I suppose there were even more of them who coughed, cried, wheezed, or squinted when they looked upon that serpent. What does that matter to us? The text is still the same, *"if a serpent had bitten any man, when he beheld the serpent of brass, he lived."*

You see, it is very possible that an Israelite could have died while *praying* to the serpent or while *swinging the door of his heart open* for the serpent to come in, for God made no promise concerning those things. But, mark this down, there was not a single Israelite who *beheld* the serpent who did not live! For, by grace they were saved through *beholding*.

Of course, Jesus is no longer on the cross for us to behold with our eyes. Rather, we see Jesus dying for us in the gospel record, with the eyes of our faith. *"For by grace are you saved through faith . . ."* (Ephesians 2:8). And, though there will be many perish who *pray*, none will perish who *believe*. For Jesus promised that *"whosoever believes in him should not perish, but have eternal life."*

Some preachers preach the cross of Christ so powerfully, but, just as the great reformer Martin Luther could not entirely free himself from his Catholic roots, these preachers also find it hard to part with things they've heard all their lives. After they have so wonderfully preached the gospel, therefore, instead of encouraging people to trust in the good news they've just heard, they will sometimes inadvertently divert people's attention away from the cross by giving them a prayer to pray.

Even if these preachers believe salvation comes through faith in the finished work of Christ, by adding a "sinner's prayer" to their gospel message, they can unintentionally cause a sinner to view the death of Christ as only a necessary *part* of their salvation, while viewing their prayer as that which actually acquires, completes, and guarantees their salvation. When people misunderstand the gospel this way, their faith will be in the fact that they prayed for salvation, instead of being in the fact that Jesus died for their sins.

I will never forget a certain weekday afternoon when I stopped by my church to pray. I had a key to the church building, and I often enjoyed going there by myself to be alone with God. But, on this particular day, when I unlocked the door, I discovered I was not alone.

As I entered the vestibule, I saw one of our associate pastors, white as a sheet, staring back at me. In his hand was a "Chick

Tract," a gospel tract that comes in the form of a little comic book. This particular tract included a step-by-step salvation plan with a "sinner's prayer" at the end.

When my associate pastor was a boy, he read the same tract he was now holding in his hand, and he prayed the "sinner's prayer" at the end of it. But he was now doubting his salvation. He was afraid that, when he was a boy, perhaps he didn't have the right knowledge, say the right words, or feel the right way when he prayed. And my associate pastor had been reading this tract over and over again, trying to remember what he did when he prayed so he could know whether or not he was truly saved.

All of this could have been avoided if that tract would have simply turned that young man's eyes to the cross and left them there. That way, instead of trying to remember what *he* did, he would have remembered what *Jesus* did. This step-by-step sinner's prayer salvation has confused so many people. Rest assured, the only steps necessary for salvation are the steps Jesus took when He walked to the place where He was crucified.

There are so many people wondering whether they repented enough, prayed the right words, or followed the right steps. They wonder, "Did I do everything right?"

Please hear me. There is only one question you need to concern yourself with, and it's not "Did I?" It's "Did *He*?" It's, "Did He (Jesus) die on the cross for me?"

Those Israelites weren't told to look at *themselves*; they were told to look at the *serpent* on the pole. Even so, Christ is telling you, *"Look unto me, and be ye saved, all the ends of the earth: for I am God, and there is none else."* (Isaiah 45:22)

The danger of the sinner's prayer is that it can cause people to fail to see Jesus' salvation as a *finished* work. In John 19:30, we are told, *"When Jesus therefore had received the vinegar, he said, It is finished: and he bowed his head, and gave up the ghost."*

Imagine that you're in trouble with the Internal Revenue Service (IRS). You have a large sum of back taxes you owe, and you have no money to pay these taxes. The IRS has begun proceedings to seize your property, and they will put you in jail for tax evasion.

One night, you are sitting alone in your house and are worried sick about this problem, when all of a sudden you hear a knock at your door. A man, who works for a very benevolent businessman in town, wants to speak with you.

"My boss heard about the terrible situation you are in, and he felt sorry for you," he says. "So, he went to the Internal Revenue Service and paid them everything you owe."

The man hands you a receipt that shows your entire balance has been paid in full. The generous businessman has satisfied the IRS on your behalf!

How do you suppose you would respond to this good news? Well, if you believed it, you would probably hold on to that receipt, thank the man, and shout for joy, right? But, let's suppose that, while you're celebrating, the man decides to add some of his *own* words to his master's message.

"All you have to do is ask my boss to come into your heart and save you from the IRS."

Wouldn't that confuse you? Not only would it be illogical, but it would infer that something else must be done in addition to paying your debt. Therefore, though you once celebrated the receipt as proof of your deliverance, you now no longer can. This is what can happen when we tell someone the good news that Jesus died to pay the penalty for their sins but then add that they must ask God to save them from those sins.

If you have prayed the "sinner's prayer" and still doubt your salvation, you should quit looking to your *prayers* and start looking to *Jesus*. Before I was saved, I set the world's record in sinner's prayers. Every time I doubted my salvation, I would say, "Lord, if I'm not saved please save me." I was so miserable. Then, one day, Pastor Spurgeon pointed me to the cross, and I saw that my salvation was finished.

When I saw Jesus suffering on that cross, I realized that salvation wasn't something I needed to ask God to do; it was something already there for me (by faith) to enjoy! Jesus said, *"If any man thirst, let him come unto me, and drink . . ."* (John 7:37). All that time, I had been like a thirsty man standing at a well *praying* for water, when I could have been *drinking* the water from the hands that dug the well.

14 THE ROMAN ROAD, PART I (OUR HEART & MOUTH)

Since the 20th Century, one of the most popular methods of sharing the gospel has been the "Roman Road to Salvation." This method was designed to lead someone to Christ by using only select passages from the book of Romans, most especially Romans 10. Interestingly, while I was writing this chapter, a church planting missionary contacted my church, seeking financial support for his ministry. When he called me, I asked him, "Can you lead someone to Christ without using the book of Romans?"

There was a long and awkward pause on the phone as he struggled for words. After pondering for some time, he finally said, *"No; I guess I can't."* This man was supposed to be an expert on evangelism—one who has been professionally trained in seminary and sent out to win the lost to Christ. But, he was unable to use the other 65 books in the Bible to lead someone to Christ.

This is very sad indeed. Even sadder, this missionary is not alone. I've spoken to several preachers who've admitted to me that they cannot lead someone to Christ without using the book of Romans, specifically Romans Chapter 10.

This forces us to face the reality that either Romans Chapter 10 is the only book God can use to save the lost, or many of our preachers today are poorly trained and are basing their evangelistic strategy on a misunderstanding of this chapter. Having grown up in an evangelistic church, I learned the "Roman Road" at an early age. As a young teenager, I had the "Roman Road" verses highlighted in my pocket New Testament, and I had paper clips marking their locations for a speedy delivery of the "salvation" message—a message that always ended with Romans 10, especially verses 9-10: *"That if you shall confess with your mouth the Lord Jesus, and shall believe in your heart that God has raised him from the dead, you shall be saved. For with the heart man believes unto righteousness; and with the mouth confession is made unto salvation."*

It seemed clear enough. Just confess with your mouth that Jesus is Lord and believe in your heart that God raised Him from the dead, and you will be saved. All my life, I believed that God raised Jesus from the dead. And I had confessed with my mouth that He was Lord.

So I assumed I was saved. But is this really what Paul was teaching? Didn't Jesus say in Matthew 7:21, *"Not everyone that says unto me, Lord, Lord, shall enter into the kingdom of heaven . . ."*?

The problem with the "Roman Road" strategy is that it gives a New Testament answer without giving an Old Testament explanation. The "Roman Road" ends with Romans 10, which is a chapter concerning Jewish people. Notice how Paul begins chapter 10: *"Brethren, my heart's desire and prayer to God for Israel is, that they might be saved."*

Unfortunately, many evangelists are unaware of the textual and historical context of Romans 10. In Romans 10, Paul was referring to an Old Testament passage in Deuteronomy 30. Therefore, to understand Romans 10, you must first understand Deuteronomy 30.

In Deuteronomy 30, God promised Israel that, if they ever went into captivity for disobeying His word, He would always deliver them out of captivity if they would repent and obey His commandments. Here's the important part: In this covenant, God warned the Jews that they knew His commandments, so they could never claim to be ignorant of them.

Here's what God told them in Deuteronomy 30:11-14: *"For this commandment which I command you this day, it is not hidden from you, neither is it far off. It is not in heaven, that you should say, Who shall go up for us to heaven, and bring it unto us, that we may hear it, and do it? Neither is it beyond the sea, that you should say, Who shall go over the sea for us, and bring it unto us, that we may hear it, and do it? But the word is very near you, in your mouth, and in your heart, that you may do it."*

God was telling the Israelites, when I punish you for not

obeying my commandments, don't say to one another, "Who will go into heaven to get God's commandments for us, that we may do them?" And don't say, "Who will travel overseas to find them for us, that we may obey them?" Why? Because God said His commandments were not far away from them. He told them, *"the word is very near you, in your mouth, and in your heart, that you may do it."*

Now, watch how Paul applies what God told Israel in Deuteronomy 30 to Jesus Christ, in Romans 10:6-8: *"Say not in your heart, Who shall ascend into heaven? (that is, to bring Christ down from above:) Or, Who shall descend into the deep? (that is, to bring up Christ again from the dead.) . . . The word is near you, [even] in your mouth, and in your heart . . ."*

Unaware that Paul is quoting from Deuteronomy 30, many evangelists believe that since Paul said, *"the word is . . . in your mouth,"* then Paul must be telling us we need to pray a sinner's prayer (with our mouths) to be saved. But listen again to what the passage in Deuteronomy says: *"But the word [the commandment] is very near you, in your mouth . . ."*

In Deuteronomy 30, God told the Jews how near His commandments were to them. He said His law wasn't something beyond them that they needed to find, but that it was something in them they needed to obey. God did not say, *"the word is in your mouth that you may say it . . ."* but rather, *"that you may do it."*

So, in Deuteronomy 30, God was not referring to a prayerful formality; He was referring to their inward familiarity. He was essentially telling the Jews, "You know my law: you have spoken it with your own mouths. You know it by heart. So, when I send you into captivity for breaking my Word, you can't claim you didn't know it." God was telling them, "If you want to be delivered from captivity, don't be asking someone to bring you the commandments; just keep the commandments you know!"

In the same way, in Romans 10, Paul is telling the Jewish people, "You have strayed from God's law, and now you are in bondage to the Roman government, and worse than that, you are in bondage to sin and death." And, like the commandments, Paul is reminding them, "You can't claim to be ignorant of Jesus Christ! You know the Messiah: He is in your mouth and in your heart!"

God's Old Testament commandments, with a legal, bloody, and sacrificial finger, had been pointing those Jews to the knowledge of Jesus Christ and to the obedience of His gospel. Every Old

Testament command and sacrifice was looking forward to Jesus and crying, *"Behold the Lamb of God, which takes away the sin of the world"* (John 1:29). So, Paul was telling the Jews, "Christ is no stranger to you! He is the same Messiah promised in the Law. He is the Savior we know in our hearts from the Old Testament Scriptures and have spoken of with our own mouths since we were children. And, *"if you shall confess with your mouth the Lord Jesus, and shall believe in your heart that God has raised him from the dead, you shall be saved"* (Romans 10:9).

The Jews knew Jesus died on the cross, but for them to believe God raised Him from the dead would require them to acknowledge Him as their Messiah, and His death as the sacrifice for their sins. And, once Israel knew Jesus as their Savior, they would finally understand that the true deliverance God promised in Deuteronomy 30 was the gospel Paul preached in Romans 10. But, not knowing the historical context of Romans 10, many evangelists are having gentiles focus on their hearts and mouths, when Paul was trying to get Jews to focus on Jesus.

Most of us have heard some preacher quote Romans 10:10 (*with the heart man believes*), and say, "To go to heaven, we must have a *heart* knowledge of Christ and not a *head* knowledge of Christ." Then, inevitably, some poor soul will begin wondering if his knowledge of Christ is in his head or in his heart when Paul's mentioning of the heart and mouth was only incidental to his mentioning of Jesus, in whom we must believe to be saved.

When we fail to interpret Romans 10 in light of its subject (Jesus), we take what God meant to be so simple, and we make it so confusing. For example,

- Jesus said in Matthew 11:15, *"He that has ears to hear, let him hear."*
- He said again in John 6:40, *"everyone who sees the Son, and believes on him, may have everlasting life . . ."*
- And, in Romans 10:10, Paul said, *"with the mouth confession is made unto salvation."*

If these scriptures are not interpreted correctly, a person could begin to wonder if he needs his *ears*, his *eyes*, his *mouth*, or a combination of all three to be saved. Likewise, by misinterpreting Romans 10, many believe they're going to heaven because they have confessed Jesus as Lord with their mouths, when (once again)

Jesus said in Matthew 7:21, *"Not every one that says unto me, Lord, Lord, shall enter into the kingdom of heaven . . ."*

Not long ago, another church planting missionary called my church seeking financial support for his ministry. When I asked him what a person had to do to be saved, he cited Romans 10:9-10 and told me we had to believe with our hearts and confess with our mouths. I then reminded the missionary about John 3:16, where Jesus said all who believe in Him shall be saved (no mention of the mouth). I then asked the missionary if a person could be saved by faith in Christ alone, or if confessing with the mouth was an additional requirement for salvation.

Unsure of the correct answer, the missionary got real quiet. But, after a little contemplation, he said, "I'm going to say we have to confess with our mouths, too." He is not alone. Other church planting missionaries have also confirmed to me that it is their belief that a person must pray, in addition to putting his or her faith in Christ. If these missionaries are correct, then Jesus either gave false or incomplete information to Nicodemus about salvation.

Furthermore, there are approximately 70,000,000 deaf people in the world, and many of them are unable to speak. If these missionary are correct, then these people cannot be saved, because they cannot confess Jesus as Lord with their mouths. And it is troubling when we realize that missionaries like this are traveling across the world teaching these doctrines to other people.

The truth is, we are saved by faith in Jesus Christ, like the Bible says. The mouth is simply one of many body members used to illustrate our inner reception or rejection of God's Word. The mouth (in and of itself) has nothing to do with us being saved. Here is a quick look at how the Holy Spirit has used many of our body parts to illustrate this very thing:

- The hardening of the *heart* (Romans 2:5)
- The stopping of the *ears* (Acts 7:57)
- The pulling away of the *shoulder* (Zechariah 7:11)
- The closing of the *eyes* (Isaiah 6:10)
- The stiffening of the *neck* (Jeremiah 17:23)
- The turning of the *foot* (Isaiah 58:13)
- The blasphemy/confession of the *mouth* (Revelation 13:6, Romans 10:9)

We must understand, then, that these are only *outward physical* illustrations used to illustrate an *inward spiritual* response.

In John 9, there is a wonderful account where Jesus, having met a blind man, spat on the ground and made clay of the spittle. Jesus then anointed the eyes of the blind man with the clay and said unto him, *"Go, wash in the pool of Siloam."* Afterward, we are told that the blind man *"went his way therefore, and washed, and came seeing."*

When the Pharisees heard the blind man had been healed, they asked him what he thought of Jesus. When the former blind man told them he believed Jesus was a prophet, the Pharisees didn't like his answer, so they cast him out of the synagogue. But when Jesus *"had found him, he said unto him, Do you believe on the Son of God? He answered and said, Who is he, Lord, that I might believe on him? And Jesus said unto him, You have both seen him, and it is he who is speaking with you. And he said, Lord, I believe. And he worshipped him"* (John 9:35-38).

Don't miss what's happening here. John 3:36, says, *"He that believes on the Son has everlasting life . . ."* And Jesus is asking this former blind man, *"Do you believe on the Son of God?"* And the man, most probably staring Jesus in the face with his newly opened eyes, asks Jesus, *"Who is he, Lord, that I might believe on him?"*

Pay close attention to how Jesus answers this man, because it is similar to our text in Romans 10: *"And Jesus said unto him, You have both seen him, and it is he who is speaking with you."* In other words, Jesus was telling him, "The Son of God is near you. He is someone you already know. He is someone you have seen with your eyes. Someone you are listening to right now with your own ears; and your eyes need only to see Him for who He is, and your ears need only to hear Him for who He claims to be." And instead of closing his eyes to the light or stopping his ears to the truth, this man yielded his ears to Jesus' words and said, *"Lord, I believe."*

Like this blind man, Jesus had already helped Israel. He led them out of Egypt. He tore down the walls of Jericho for them. He gave them the covenants, and He died for them on the cross. All Paul was trying to do was get Israel to see Jesus for who he was so they could believe in Him for the salvation they needed.

Don't let the Devil use passages like Romans 10 to distract you from the person they are speaking of. I suppose I will never forget visiting a particular church near Ft. Worth, Texas, one Sunday night. It was my first time to visit the church, so one of the church members (recognizing me as a first-time visitor) came over to welcome me. After introducing himself, the church member had a question for me.

"If you were to die tonight, where would you go?"

"I would go to heaven."

"How do you know?"

"I know I am going to heaven because Jesus Christ died for my sins on the cross, and my faith is in Him."

The man accepted my answer and began to walk away. But, I stopped him. "Now I want to ask you a question: If you were to die tonight, where would you go?"

"I would go to heaven."

"How do you know?"

"Well, what you said; but, do you know Romans 10:9-10?"

"Yes."

"Well, I've done all that; that's how I know I'm going to heaven."

"I've done all that . . ." Do you see the vast yet subtle difference between our answers? My assurance was based on something *Christ* had done. His assurance was based on something *he* had done. But what that man told me is exactly what I would have told him, had he asked me the same question a few years earlier, before I was saved.

If you have followed Romans 10:9-10 but still doubt your salvation, then it is probably because you have placed your faith in what you have done with your *mouth* and *heart*, instead of placing it in what Jesus has done with your *sin*. The former believes on what you have done; the latter believes on Jesus.

Jesus asked that blind man only one question: *"Do you believe on the Son of God?"* because Jesus knew that man's salvation did not depend on what he did with his eyes, or with his ears, or with his mouth, but on what he did with *the Son of God*.

What about you: Do you believe on the Son of God?

15 THE ROMAN ROAD, PART II (CALLING ON THE LORD)

Another misunderstood passage on the "Roman Road" is Romans 10:13: *"For whosoever shall call upon the name of the Lord shall be saved."* This verse promises salvation to everyone who *"calls upon the name of the Lord."* And, according to sinner's prayer evangelists, *"calling upon the name of the Lord"* means to ask God to save you. But is this really what it means to call upon the name of the Lord?

When I was a young man, Romans 10:13 was given to me as assurance that, if I had sincerely asked God to save me, then I was most certainly saved. But I later learned that wasn't necessarily true. In fact, when we read about someone calling on the name of the Lord in the Bible, it is almost always referring to mature Christians who are acknowledging God for who He is and relying upon His provision. For example, in the book of Genesis we read of Abraham calling upon the name of the Lord on at least three separate occasions (Genesis 12:8, 13:4, 21:33); and, on neither occasion was Abraham asking God to save him.

So, what does it mean to *"call upon the name of the Lord"*? Let's read Romans 10:11-13 carefully and see:

> (11) *For the scripture says, Whosoever believes on him shall not be ashamed.* (12) *For there is no difference between the Jew and the Greek: for the same Lord over all is rich unto all that call upon him.* (13) *For whosoever shall call upon the name of the Lord shall be saved.*

Notice how Paul is using "believing on" and "calling upon" interchangeably. This is because "believing" and "calling" are essentially the same thing. In each verse we just read, there is a subject, a verb, a preposition, and a direct object. If you don't mind marking in this book (or your Bible), grab a pen, and be ready to mark each of these categories as we go.

First, we will look at the subject in these verses. In verse 11, underline the word "*Whosoever*". Whosoever tells us salvation is for anybody who wants it. Likewise, in verse 12, the subject is "*all*". Underscore the word "all" in verse 12, for God wants all to be saved. In verse 13, the subject again is "*whosoever.*" Underline "whosoever" in verse 13. So, make no mistake about it: salvation is for anyone who wants it. If you want to go to heaven, you can!

Now let's look at the verb in these verses—the action you (the subject) must take to be saved. In verse 11, underline the word "*believes.*" So, *whosoever*—all who want to be saved must *believe*. This perfectly lines up with the rest of the Bible, such as Acts 13:39, which says, *"And by him* [Jesus] *all* [our subject] *that believe* [the action we must take] *are justified* [saved] . . ."

As the verb in verse 11 was "believes," so the verb in verse 12 is "*call.*" Underscore the word "call" in verse 12. In verse 13, the verb again is "*call.*" Do you see how Paul is using "believe" and "call" interchangeably here?

By adding the verb "call," God is not giving you something else to do to be saved (in addition to believing). Instead, He is giving you a better understanding of the word "believes".

The Greek word ἐπικαλέομαι (epikaleomai – ep-ee-kal-eh'-om-ahee), translated "call upon" implies more than our English translation offers. If we want to know what the apostle Paul meant by epikaleomai (call upon), all we have to do is watch how Paul used this word in Acts 25:11. Listen to what Paul told a judge, while in court, *to be saved* from accusations made against him:

> For if I be an offender, or have committed any thing worthy of death, I refuse not to die: but if there be none of these things whereof these accuse me, no man may deliver me unto them. I appeal unto Caesar.

Paul was afraid that Festus, a Roman judge, was about to deliver him into the hands of people who wanted to kill him. So, knowing his rights under Roman law, Paul invoked a right afforded to every Roman citizen and appealed his case to a higher court. Paul said, *"I appeal unto Caesar."*

The Greek word translated "appeal" here is the same word translated "call upon/on" in Romans 10:12-13. And Paul is using this word to invoke his legal right to appeal his case (to Caesar). God willing, we shall now see how "call upon" and "believe" are the same thing.

Many times in Scripture, the idea of *calling* or *believing* is simply referred to as *faith*. In fact, the Bible uses many descriptions for faith. But, whether it is described as repentance, trusting, receiving, resting, calling, or believing, it's all the same thing—it's faith. For example, when the apostle Paul appealed his case to Caesar, it was all the same as him believing in Caesar, because Paul was *relying* (believing) on Caesar's judgment.

Now that we've considered the subject and verb in our Romans 10 verses, let's take a look at the preposition. One of a preposition's functions is to send the action to the place it should go, such as a direct object. When Paul said, *"I appeal unto Caesar."* "I" would be the subject; "appeal" would be the verb, *"unto"* would be the preposition, and *"Caesar"* would be the direct object (because Caesar is the one the appeal is going to).

So, in Romans 10:11, "whosoever" is the subject; "believes" is the verb, and *"on"* is the preposition. In verse 11, underline the word "on." In verse 12, the preposition is "upon" (a synonym for on), and in verse 13 it is (once again) "upon."

Let's recap. The word "Whosoever" means anyone may be saved. The words "Believes" and "call" mean we must have faith—we must believe, appeal our case, etc. to be saved. But the word "on" or "upon," tells us that our faith must rely *on* something—our appeal must be based *on* something.

If an appeal is not based on legal grounds, it will be powerless to overturn a guilty verdict. In the same way, if a person's faith is not based on legal grounds, it will be powerless to overturn sin. Faith in a false bridge can send a man into the river, and faith in a false gospel can send a man to hell. Faith is no greater than the object it's placed in.

So let's consider the object of our faith. No matter where you look in scripture, salvation's subject will always be some form of *whosoever;* salvation's action will always be some form of *faith,* and salvation's object will always be someone named *Jesus*.

Look now in verse 11 and draw a big line under the word "him." Again, in verse 12, it is "him." And, in verse 13, it is the name of the "Lord." Why? Because the Bible says of Jesus, *"Neither is there salvation in any other: for there is none other name under heaven given among men, whereby we must be saved"* (Acts 4:12).

So, in Romans 10:13 we read, *"For whosoever shall call upon the name of the Lord shall be saved."* The *"name of the Lord"* refers to the power of the Lord to forgive us of our sins. When an officer refers to his legal power, he may tell someone to stop in the "name of the law." Even so, when referring to the power of the gospel, the *name of the Lord* speaks of Jesus' power to forgive sins through the sacrifice He made.

When Paul appealed his case to Caesar, he was invoking a legal right offered to him by the law. And, having made his appeal, Paul showed that he had accepted Caesar's authority and was now relying on (believing/calling on) on Caesar's judgment.

As a sinner, you won't stand before a Roman judge; you will stand justly condemned before God. But, *"whosoever shall call upon the name of the Lord shall be saved* [from that condemnation].*"* This is because every person has a legal right offered to them by the Gospel. They have the right to appeal their case to Jesus, who died in their place.

In an American court, there is a practice called "judicial notice." It's when a court of law accepts a fact, without hearing arguments from either side, when the court has prior knowledge of the fact. When we appeal our case to Jesus, God takes judicial notice that Jesus has paid our penalty. And, upon deliberation of this fact, He announces His ruling: *"He that believes on him is not condemned . . ."* (John 3:18).

All who appeal their case to Jesus shall be saved, *"for the same Lord over all is rich unto all that call upon him. For whosoever shall call upon the name of the Lord shall be saved."* (Romans 10:12-13)

ALL – the subject
CALL – the action
UPON – the preposition
HIM – the object

Call upon Him! Friend, there is an unholy Devil and a most-holy law that stand validly in heaven's court to accuse you to the Judge. If you're honest, you'll plead guilty as charged. But if you're wise, you'll appeal your case to Jesus.

After an attorney has made his final argument, you may hear him say, "I rest my case." Reader, make the cross of Christ your final argument. Plead guilty; then rest your case on Jesus.

16 WHAT IF I'M NOT ONE OF THE ELECT?

Calvinists believe that God, in eternity past, looked down through the ages of time and, seeing every person He would ever create, sovereignly chose to save some of those people, and to condemn the rest. Those fortunate enough to be chosen for salvation [so they say], are called the elect; and, according to them, only these elect people can be saved. In order to save these elect people, Calvinists believe God sent His only begotten Son into the world to die for their sins and *for their sins alone*. So, according to Calvinists, if you're not chosen to be saved, then Jesus didn't die for you, and therefore you cannot be saved.

There were some fine men of God who embraced Calvinism during the Reformation era, and their teachings have been embraced by many fine men of God today. But, with all due respect to these great men, there is a great problem with their teaching.

In 1 Corinthians 15:3, the apostle Paul said, *"For I delivered unto you first of all that which I also received, how that Christ died for our sins according to the scriptures..."*

The word gospel means "good news." And Paul said the good news he received was that *"Christ died for our sins..."* Not only did Paul receive the good news that *"Christ died for our sins..,"* but Paul said he preached that same good news to others.

"Christ died for our sins." That is good news! But suppose the apostle Paul preached the "good news" according to the Calvinists. Could you imagine Paul telling the Corinthian people: "You people

of Corinth, I have good news for you: God may have sent His Son, Jesus, to die for your sins!'"?

I can just imagine Paul telling them, "Although Jesus may not have died for your sins, you should still believe in him, or you will be condemned if you don't. For, the scripture says, *"he that believes not is condemned . . ."* (John 3:18).

Imagine someone in the audience saying, "I would like to believe this good news, but how do I know whether or not Jesus died for me?"

"Only God knows who Jesus died for sir," Paul might answer. "But, the good news is, God has either chosen to *save* you or to *condemn* you. You are either one of God's elect or you are not. And, you should believe in Jesus as your Savior, even though He may not be."

I don't know about you, but I am so glad God didn't give us such a complicated message as that. Like a doctor telling you that you have a fifty-fifty chance to live, the Calvinists' message may give you hope, but it can hardly give you assurance because one may always be left to wonder whether or not he or she is truly one of God's elect, and thus to wonder if he or she is truly saved.

I am not about to tell you that the doctrine of election is not in the Bible. Election is in the Bible, but the Calvinists' view on election differs from what the Bible teaches. In fact, when the doctrine of election is properly understood, it will comfort the people of God, not confuse them.

It's not the doctrine of election that causes doubt; it's the misunderstanding of it. Let me explain. Many people understand election as a time when God arbitrarily selected to save a limited number of people by His grace and to allow the unfortunate majority to hopelessly die in their sin. This teaching is very disturbing to me.

I have heard so many Christians ignorantly say, "I don't know why God chose to save me," perhaps leaving others to wonder why God may not have chosen to save them. And, if you are afraid that you may not be one of God's elect, I would like to take God's precious Word and put your fears to rest. In this chapter, I will give you three ways you can know, without a shadow of a doubt, that you can be saved.

First, you can be saved because Jesus died for you. There is one thing in this life that can never be taken away from you: it is the fact that Jesus Christ died on the cross for you. Romans 5:6 is one of my favorite verses in the Word of God:

> *"For when we were yet without strength, in due time Christ died for the ungodly."*

Whom did Christ die for? He died for the *"ungodly."* Reader, are you ungodly? Do your sins make you unacceptable to God? If you are ungodly, then rest assured, Christ died for you; for here it is plainly written in God's Word: *"Christ died for the ungodly."*

"Oh, [a Calvinist may argue] but Christ only died for the ungodly elect."

Well, that would be fine if that's what the Bible said, but it doesn't say Christ died for the ungodly elect; it says Christ died for the ungodly. And, should there remain any doubt who Christ died for, Romans 5:18 should settle this matter once for all:

> *Therefore as by the offence of one judgment came upon all men to condemnation; even so by the righteousness of one the free gift came upon all men unto justification of life.*

In the above verse, the Bible clearly says as JUDGMENT came upon *"all men"* through Adam. This much we all agree on. But the Bible goes on to say the FREE GIFT [of salvation] came upon *"all men"* through Christ. So, if Calvinists define the words *"all men"* to mean *salvation* came only upon all elect men, then they must also interpret these words to mean *judgment* came only upon all elect men. And, if judgment came only upon the elect, then the non-elect don't need salvation, because judgment never came upon them.

But, once again, the Scripture says exactly what it means: *"as by the offence of one judgment came upon all men to condemnation; even so by the righteousness of one the free gift came upon all men unto justification of life."* So, you can know that you can be saved by knowing Jesus died for you—by knowing that as judgment came upon you to condemnation in Adam, *"even so"*, the free gift of salvation came upon you in Jesus Christ.

Another way you can know you can be saved is by knowing that Jesus came to save you. 1 Timothy 1:15 says, *"This is a faithful saying, and worthy of all acceptation, that Christ Jesus came into the world to save sinners...*" Are you a sinner? The Bible says *"Christ Jesus came into the world to save sinners..."* So, if you can say with confidence that you are a sinner, then you can say with confidence that Jesus came into the world to save you.

Now, that's what I call good news! The apostle Paul said this is to be considered faithful and worthy of all acceptation. So, it's time for you to accept the fact that Christ Jesus came into the world to save *you* because that's what the Bible says He came to do.

Lastly, you can know you can be saved not only because Jesus died to save you, and not only because Jesus came to save you, but by knowing that Jesus wants to save you. The apostle Peter said, *"The Lord is... not willing that any should perish, but that all should come to repentance"* (2 Peter 3:9).

You see, God doesn't want anybody to go to hell. In Ezekiel 33:11, God said, *"As I live, says the Lord God, I have no pleasure in the death of the wicked; but that the wicked turn from his way and live: turn you, turn you from your evil ways; for why will you die...?"*

In this verse, God said He doesn't want wicked people to die. He wants them to turn and live. But I believe the most remarkable thing about this verse is the question God asked toward the end: He asked, *"why will you die?"*

That's a good question: Why would you die when you can live? Do you see now, friend? You don't have to die! Jesus said in John 6:47, *"He that believes on me has everlasting life."*

Jesus *came* to save you. Jesus *died* to save you. And Jesus *wants* to save you. So, why would you die, when you can believe on Jesus and live?

You may be thinking, "If God really wants to save everybody, then what are the verses on election talking about?" Let me explain. Election is God's selection concerning salvation. Election is God, by His own sovereign will, electing to save everyone who will come to Him through faith in His Son Jesus, and to condemn everyone who will not.

Election is not so much about God putting a limit on *how many* people will go to heaven as it is God putting a limit on *how they'll get there*. God chose to provide the world only one way to be saved, and that way is Jesus Christ. Jesus said, *"I am the way..."* (John 14:6). We must choose to take that "way" for ourselves.

In Deuteronomy 30:19, God told Israel, *"I call heaven and earth to record this day against you, that I have set before you life and death, blessing and cursing: therefore choose life, that both you and your descendants may live . . ."*

In the above verse, notice how God elected life for Israel, but not everyone in Israel elected life for themselves. This is confirmed to us in Isaiah 45:4, where God said, *"For Jacob my servant's sake, and Israel mine elect, I have even called you by your name: I have surnamed you, though you have not known me."*

In the Old Testament book of Genesis, God preached the gospel to Abraham, and Abraham was saved by faith in that gospel message. Today, we are saved the same way. And all who believe Abraham's gospel are part of Abraham's family.

Here's how the apostle Paul explains this in Galatians 3:7-9, *"Know then that it is those of faith who are the sons of Abraham. And the Scripture, foreseeing that God would justify the Gentiles by faith, preached the gospel beforehand to Abraham, saying, "In you shall all the nations be blessed." So then, those who are of faith are blessed with faithful Abraham."*

So, according to God's covenant with Abraham, those who come to God through faith in Christ are the seed of Abraham—the chosen ones of God. This truth is confirmed to us in Isaiah 41:8, where God said, *"But you, Israel, are my servant, Jacob whom I have chosen, the seed of Abraham my friend."*

So, you see, God's election is more about *Jesus* than it is about *you.* Jesus is God's elect, thus everyone who believes in Him is part of God's election. Galatians 3:29, says, *"And if you are Christ's, then you are Abraham's seed, and heirs according to the promise."*

I believe, therefore, that the simplest way for us to understand election is to understand that, in eternity past, God chose (elected) to save the world through Jesus Christ, and through Him alone. The apostle John said, *"He that has the Son has life; and he that has not the Son of God has not life"* (1John 5:12).

So, the problem with election isn't that God hasn't chosen many people for Jesus; it's that many people haven't chosen Jesus for themselves. Therefore, if you want to be one of God's elect, come take Jesus as your Savior. For Jesus said in John 6:37, *"he who comes to me I will in no way cast out."*

17 WHAT IS SAVING FAITH?

In John 6:47, Jesus said, *"Truly, truly, I say to you, He that believes on me has everlasting life."* Many people are absolutely certain Jesus died for them on the cross. They believe in the salvation of Jesus, and they esteem the Word of God to be faithful and true. But, although they believe these things, they are still unsure if they are saved, because they fear there may be something wrong with their faith. These people repeatedly ask themselves questions, such as:

- "What if my faith isn't strong enough?"
- "What if I don't understand well enough?"
- "What if I don't believe in Jesus the right way?"

In other words, when they should be resting in Jesus, they are questioning themselves, fearing their faith is not "saving faith"— the kind (or quality) of faith that can actually save them.

When people question their faith, it is often due to something confusing they've heard in church. For example, when I grew up, I used to hear preachers say, "The distance between heaven and hell is the distance between your head and your heart." They would go on to explain, saying, "To go to heaven, you must have a heart knowledge of Christ, instead of a head knowledge of Christ." Then, all these poor people were left to wonder if their knowledge of Jesus was in their head or in their heart.

Some preachers even teach that God commands us to question our faith, quoting 2 Corinthians 13:5 as their grounds for doing so, which says, *"Examine yourselves, whether you be in the faith; prove your own selves. Know you not your own selves, how that Jesus Christ is in you, except you be reprobates?"*

After quoting this verse, they will tell the church, "The Bible says, we all need to 'examine' ourselves to see if we are 'in the faith' and prove that Jesus Christ is in us." As a result, people will feel compelled to question (examine) their faith in Christ.

While I certainly believe every person should soberly consider his relationship with God, I do not believe Paul was teaching this type of fearful and fruitless introspection. When Paul encouraged the Corinthians to examine themselves, it was not to make them question their salvation. It was to make them certain of Paul's ministry.

The Corinthians had begun to question Paul's authority. So, in 2 Corinthians 13:3, Paul said, *"Since you seek a proof of Christ speaking in me . . ."* In other words, if you're looking for evidence of Christ speaking in me, then *examine yourselves*. I believe Paul is saying, "Since you were saved under my ministry, then you are the biggest proof of Christ speaking in me."

Improperly taught verses like this, among other things, can confuse people about the matter of faith and cause them to fear that their faith may not be the "real thing." But, rest assured, you can know that your faith is genuine saving faith. And, by God's grace, I will show you how in this chapter. But, before I explain what "saving" faith is, let me first clarify what salvation is.

Salvation means God, 2,000 years ago, saved you from the awful and eternal consequences of your sin. God accomplished this salvation by sending Jesus to basically do three things for you:
1. Perfectly keep God's commandments on your behalf.
2. Pay your penalty for breaking God's commandments by dying (on the cross) in your place.
3. Overcome death for you by being raised from the dead on your behalf.

So, when Christ died on the cross, He was taking full responsibility for every sin He knew you would ever commit, and He saved you from the condemnation of that sin by being condemned in your place. Since Jesus did all this for you 2,000 years ago, this means your salvation is already accomplished.

Our salvation was accomplished in Christ, therefore, long before you and I were ever born, and thus, it was accomplished completely apart from us and completely apart from our faith (we weren't alive yet, so our faith didn't exist). So, you are not saved by your faith; you are saved by Jesus.

When people seek assurance of their salvation by examining their faith, they will often begin to doubt. Like a ship in a storm, the sailor doesn't get assurance by considering his anchor on the ship, but by considering the rock upon which his anchor rests. Similarly, we do not gain assurance by examining our faith but by examining the Rock upon which our faith rests (Jesus).

You may be thinking, *"But, I thought the Bible says we are saved by faith."* Well, we are only saved by faith in the sense that we are relying on (believing on) the salvation Jesus accomplished. If I use a glass of water to take medicine, then my wellness does not depend on the sufficiency of the glass, but of the medicine. Even so, if I believe in Jesus, then my salvation is no longer a question of whether my faith is sufficient, but if Jesus is sufficient. Don't look to your faith for assurance; look to Jesus for assurance, as Isaiah 45:22 says: *"Look unto me, and be you saved, all the ends of the earth: for I am God, and there is none else."*

In John 6:40, Jesus said, *"And this is the will of him that sent me, that everyone who sees the Son, and believes on him, should have everlasting life . . ."* This means you will only find peace when you look for it in Jesus. If you ever let the Devil trick you into looking at your faith, you will always find some fault with it. This is because you are an imperfect person, and imperfect people will always have an imperfect faith.

You don't need a perfect faith; you just need a perfect Savior. You just need to take your imperfect faith and place it in the perfect Son of God. Again, Jesus said, *"this is the will of Him that sent me, that everyone who sees the Son, and believes on him, may have everlasting life . . ."* So, quit looking at you; quit looking at how well you're looking; start looking at Jesus!

I was talking to a man with OCD (Obsessive Compulsive Disorder) once. This man was always worried that there was something wrong with his faith. And I told him something that seemed to help him, so I will share it with you.

I told him that faith is like gravity. Gravity causes all of us to stand somewhere. We don't just float around in space. Instead, gravity holds us down, causing all of us to stand in one place at any given time.

Similarly, faith causes all of us to stand on something. Like gravity, the law of faith pulls on every individual. We are all standing on something; it's just a matter of *where* we stand.

Some people stand on their belief that there is no God. Others stand on their works. And others stand on various religions. Personally, I stand on the gospel of Jesus Christ. When it comes to salvation, it's not a matter of *how* we stand but *where* we stand that counts.

Suppose a great fire is raging across a field. A man standing in the dry brush would surely be burned. But if a man was wise, he would start a fire in front of him, with his back to the wind. Then, after the wind carries the fire away, he would stand where the fire had already burned. By doing this, he would be safe when the fire came, because fire cannot pass where it has already burned.

The Bible tells us in Hebrews 12:29 that *"our God is a consuming fire."* Presently, God's holy and righteous fire is raging against sinners, and it is coming their way. But, on the cross, God's fiery wrath fell on Jesus. A wise man, therefore, will go to the cross and stand where the fire has already burned.

When escaping the fire, you need not concern yourself with how well you are standing. As far as your safety is concerned, you only need to know that you are standing *where the fire has already passed*. In the same way, when escaping God's fiery wrath, you need not concern yourself with how well you are standing (believing). You only need to know that you are standing at the cross—where the fire of God's judgment has already passed.

But, I can hear someone say, "I am not sure my faith understands enough for me to be saved! There is so much I still do not know!" Yes; we all have much learning to do. But a person does not need much knowledge to be saved.

When I was a small boy, I remember going to a friend's house for a swim party. The only problem was, I didn't know how to swim. When I entered the backyard, I was directed to the shallow end of the pool, which was clearly marked by a rope.

Unfortunately, however, I didn't know what the rope meant, so I eventually crossed under it, and ventured toward the deep end of the pool where the other kids were playing. To this day, I still get a sick feeling in my stomach when I remember what it felt like as I helplessly sank down into the deep water. The only thing I knew to do was to hold my breath.

While under the water, I opened my eyes and saw my friend enter the middle of the pool with a splash. He had just dived off the diving board and had no idea of the danger I was in. Still holding my breath, I saw my friend swim to the side of the pool where the ladder was. Fortunately for me, as my friend began climbing up the ladder to get out of the pool, one of his feet, for a brief moment, passed within my reach. And, to his surprise, I took hold of his ankle and was pulled to safety before I drowned.

As an adult, I have often thought back on how close I came to death that day, and I have thanked God for sending that boy my way to keep me from dying. If my hands could have saved me, they would have swum for me. But my hands didn't know how. So, they did something else: they took hold of someone who *could* swim—someone who God, in His love, sent to me that I might be saved.

When I took hold of my friend's foot, I didn't know my remaining oxygen level or the depth of the water I was in. I didn't know the water's temperature, and I didn't understand the principles of buoyancy. The only thing I knew was, God had provided that foot to me as a way to escape, and I would die in the water if I didn't take hold of it.

Like my hand, faith is not as much comprehending salvation as it is apprehending it. Faith is not limited to people who understand the depth of Scripture, but to those who know that God (by sending them Jesus) has provided them a way to escape, and that they will die in their sin if they do not take hold of Him. Saving faith is not so much an educated mind as it is a motivated hand—a hand that sees the cross within your reach and lays hold of the nail-pierced foot of Jesus before you die.

Maybe you're concerned that your faith is not *strong* enough. There may have been a time when you stood at the cross in full assurance that you were saved. But something has happened since then. Maybe you have fallen into sin. Maybe your mind has been assaulted by the Devil. Now your hand trembles at the cross, and you fear your faith does not hold onto Jesus tight enough.

Maybe you are a new believer. You have faith in Jesus, but it seems as weak and thin as a spider's silk. And you believe that if only your faith was like iron, locked and chained to Jesus, then you would feel safe. Oh friend, remember, your faith does not save you; Jesus saves you. And, though your faith is as weak as a bruised reed or a smoldering fire, which appears so vulnerable and capable of dying out, if it's placed in Jesus alone, it might as well have the strength of a steel rod and the heat of the sun itself.

Take courage! The Bible says in Romans 5:6 that it was when we were *"without strength"* that Christ died for the ungodly.

Again, in John 6:37, Jesus said, *". . . the one who comes to Me I will in no way cast out.*" It doesn't matter to God whether we come *leaping* to Jesus, *walking* to Jesus, *crawling* to Jesus, or even if we're so weak we must, like the lame man, be *carried* to Jesus; it only matters that we come to Jesus. The reason for this lies in the nature of what faith is.

Faith, in and of itself, is nothing. Faith is merely your hope—your reliance upon one thing or another. Having no substance in itself, therefore, your faith can only be measured by the substance your faith is in. Hebrews 11:1 says, *"faith is the substance of things hoped for . . ."* If your faith is in the salvation of Jesus Christ, therefore, you have saving faith.

Listen to what God said in Leviticus 1:1-4:

> *And the Lord called unto Moses, and spake unto him out of the tabernacle of the congregation, saying, Speak unto the children of Israel, and say unto them, If any man of you bring an offering unto the Lord, you shall bring your offering of the cattle, even of the herd, and of the flock. If his offering be a burnt sacrifice of the herd, let him offer a male without blemish: he shall offer it of his own voluntary will at the door of the tabernacle of the congregation before the Lord. And he shall put his hand upon the head of the burnt offering; and it shall be accepted for him to make atonement for him.*

In this passage, God told Moses that, when an Israelite brought an offering unto the Lord, that man was to put his hand on the head of the sacrificed animal. And, when he did, that animal would be accepted as an atonement for him. Listen again to verse 4, *"And he shall put his hand upon the head of the burnt offering; and it shall be accepted for him to make atonement for him."*

Why did God credit the sacrifice to the man when he placed his hand on it? Because, when the man placed his hand on the animal, he was identifying himself with it. Identification by the placement of the hand is a very common principle.

Think about it. What do we usually do when we want to have our photograph taken with someone? We get close to that person, and we put our hand somewhere on that person's shoulder or back, right? And what does that signify? It signifies our willingness to identify ourselves with that person.

Likewise, in the Old Testament, when someone offered a sacrifice to God, he would lay his hand on the animal to be sacrificed, signifying his identification with that animal and that animal's identification with him. And, seeing that the man had associated himself with that sacrifice, God credited the man's *sins* to the animal and credited the animal's *innocence* to the man (atonement). And the man's sins were forgiven.

God made no mention of the *strength* of the man's hand but the *placement* of it. If he was a strong man, who could grip the sacrifice with great strength, or if he was a feeble man, who could barely lay his trembling hand on it, God's promise was still the same: *"he shall put his hand upon the head of the burnt offering; and it shall be accepted for him to make atonement for him."*

Of course, those Old Testament sacrifices could not take away sin. They were just a symbol of Jesus' sacrifice that would come in the New Testament. And Jesus (our sacrifice) is no longer on the cross, so there is no way for us to physically go there to lay our hand on Him.

Rather, in the New Testament, our *faith* is the hand we lay on the sacrifice, when we rely on Jesus as the sacrifice for our sin. And God, seeing that we have identified ourselves with His sacrifice, credits our sin to Jesus (on the cross) and credits Jesus' righteousness to us (atonement). And our sins are forgiven.

In the Old Testament, they placed their hand on the sacrifice. In the New Testament, we place our faith on the sacrifice. What, then, is saving faith? Jesus said, *"He who believes on me has everlasting life"* (John 6:47). So, the hand (faith) that's placed on Jesus is saving faith!

In Matthew 17:20, Jesus said, *"If you have faith as a grain of mustard seed, you shall say unto this mountain, Move from here to there; and it shall remove; and nothing shall be impossible unto you."* Therefore, you don't need to be afraid. You just need to take your feeble, weak, and ignorant faith and place your faith where God placed your sin: on Jesus.

Whether you come leaping or you come lame, just come to Jesus. And He shall be accepted as your atonement. Just believe God's Word, and, like the old hymn goes, say to Jesus:

"Just as I am, though tossed about,

KNOWING I'M SAVED

with many a conflict—many a doubt,
fightings within, and fears without,
oh Lamb of God I come! I come!"

18 WHAT IS THE WITNESS OF THE SPIRIT?

The Spirit Himself bears witness with our spirit that we are the children of God. (Romans 8:16)

What exactly does Romans 8:16 mean? Many people think the witness of the Spirit is a special feeling God gives to assure us we are saved. Is there really a certain feeling we are supposed to have? And, if so, how do we know what it's supposed to feel like? And how can we know that the feeling is from God and not some counterfeit feeling from the Devil?

In this chapter, let's remove the mystery of Romans 8:16. Only by knowing what the Bible says about the witness of the Spirit can we know the specific witness we are supposed to have. As we look in God's Word, we will see that the witness of the Spirit is not so much *how* the Holy Spirit bears witness to our spirit but *who* the Holy Spirit bears witness of.

I remember listening to a preacher one night who was teaching on the witness of the Spirit. In his sermon, he said he knew for certain that he was saved. But the preacher said his wife never understood how he knew. She asked him, "How can you know you are saved?"

His wife was looking for answers. She wanted to know that she was saved. He said he told her, "Honey, it's not something I can explain; it's something I just know."

The answer he gave her may have been voiced with confidence, but it was shrouded in mystery. *It's something I just know.* To a woman searching for the assurance of her salvation, this answer was no help at all, and it must have been very bewildering for her to hear.

I am sure she wondered why God wasn't giving her that same "unexplainable" confidence. With all due respect, if a preacher cannot explain how salvation can be known, he probably has no business preaching salvation. Assurance of salvation is rooted in the Word of God, and we are called to explain the Scriptures, not mystify them.

By making the witness of the Spirit out to be something it's not, we will cause people to either have a false confidence in unexplainable feelings or a lack of confidence in biblical facts. Neither is good. Let's take a close look at Romans 8:16 now, so we can see what the witness of the Spirit is: *"The Spirit Himself..."*

The Holy Spirit Himself is the person who bears witness to us. Never base your salvation upon the testimony of another person. Nobody can tell you that you are saved but God Himself. But how does God tell us we're saved? Look at the verse again. Paul said He *"bears witness."*

To *bear witness* means to give testimony as a witness (such as a witness in a court of law). The first time we see this term used in the Bible is in the Ten Commandments, where we are told not bear false *witness* against our neighbor. Generally speaking, that means we are not to perjure ourselves by giving false testimony as a witness against an innocent person. So, when you think of the Holy Spirit bearing witness, it may help if you think of a witness stand, and of the Holy Spirit providing credible testimony to the fact of your salvation.

Immediately, therefore, this does away with the mistaken idea that the witness of the Holy Spirit is some mysterious feeling. The gospel isn't based on feelings; the gospel is based on fact. Our assurance, therefore, is always based on the factual testimony given to us in God's Word.

Just think about it. How important do you suppose an eyewitness would be in a murder case? What if a prosecutor had someone on the witness stand who could provide sworn testimony to the fact that he saw the defendant kill his wife? I would say that would be pretty important to the case. Wouldn't you?

Or, what if there was an *ear* witness? What if someone could testify that they *heard* the defendant say he killed his wife? That would be pretty important, too. Right?

But, what if the prosecutor had a *heart* witness? What if there was someone who could give sworn testimony that he *felt* in his heart that the defendant killed his wife? What if the prosecuting attorney said, "Your Honor, I would now like to call my star witness, Mr. Jones, to testify in this case."? He calls Mr. Jones to the stand and says, "Mr. Jones, I understand that you are a heart witness to this crime. Could you please tell the jury what you know about this case?"

Mr. Jones turns to the jury. "Ladies and gentlemen of the jury, I am absolutely certain that this man murdered his wife!"

The jury gasps, the audience begins to whisper, and the judge starts pounding his gavel to call the court back into order.

The prosecutor grins confidently. "I pass the witness."

If you know anything about law, then you know the statement Mr. Jones just made is a conclusive statement. A conclusive statement is a statement which offers a conclusion without providing the basis of knowledge upon which that conclusion rests. A true witness, on the other hand, will testify to his basis of knowledge, and then the jury will develop their own conclusion upon that basis.

Therefore, if the prosecutor wants to convince the jury that his star witness has told the truth, then the witness must not only tell the jury *that* he knows the defendant killed his wife but *how* he knows the defendant killed his wife.

When it's time for the defense to cross-examine the witness, the defense attorney asks him, "Mr. Jones, how do you know my client murdered his wife?"

Mr. Jones turns to the jury and says, "I cannot tell you how I know this man murdered his wife; it's not something I can explain; it's something I just know, because I feel it in my heart."

I believe you would agree that the prosecutor just lost his case. The testimony of feelings can never yield proof beyond a reasonable doubt. As we need facts to sway the jury, so you need facts to sway your heart and convince your mind. Facts give our faith something to rest on, and this is why the Holy Spirit bears witness to the facts of our salvation—the salvation Jesus accomplished for me and you.

Let's look back at our text again. The Bible says His Spirit bears witness ". . . *with our spirit.*" Some translations render this "to" our spirit instead of "with" our spirit. The Greek word translated "with" here has the idea of being a confirming (corroborating) testimony, testifying to us, *"that we are the children of God..."*

So, the Holy Spirit gives confirming testimony to the fact that we are the children of God. But what does the Holy Spirit say to us? What specific facts does He "testify" to that sways and convinces us that we are His children? To answer this question, we need to look a little further in God's Word:

In John 15:26, Jesus said, *"But when the Comforter is come, whom I will send unto you from the Father, [even] the Spirit of truth, which proceeds from the Father, He shall testify of me..."*

Jesus said, *"He shall testify of me..."* So, the Holy Spirit testifies to us concerning the facts of Jesus Christ! We see then, that God does not testify to us with mystical emotions. He testifies to us with a real assurance of salvation based on who Jesus is and on what Jesus has done.

The witness of the Spirit, therefore, leads a believer in Christ to the conclusion that Jesus' death has made him free. The Holy Spirit testifies to our spirit of the substitutionary sacrifice of Jesus, thus convincing us that we have a full pardon in His blood, and persuading us that, by Christ living and dying in our place, we are accepted by God in Him—we are the children of God. So, the witness of the Holy Spirit is when God assures us of our salvation through the testimony of Jesus Christ and the sacrifice He made.

The New Testament often refers to sacrifices as "gifts," such as in Matthew 23:19, when Jesus said, *"You fools and blind: for which is greater, the gift, or the altar that sanctifies the gift?"*

Understanding this, let's read in Hebrews 11:4 and see how God testified concerning Abel (Adam and Eve's son), bearing witness of the sacrifice Abel offered: *"By faith Abel offered unto God a more excellent sacrifice than Cain, by which he obtained witness that he was righteous, God testifying of his gifts..."*

Here is how it works: When a sinner believes the gospel message, he accepts Christ as the sacrifice for his sin. Having placed his faith in Christ's sacrifice, the Holy Spirit testifies to him that the gift (sacrifice) of Jesus has satisfied God on his account.

Everything you need for salvation is wrapped up in Jesus Christ. Salvation (including the assurance of it) is never transferred out of Jesus' jurisdiction. When a believer thinks on Christ's death, the Holy Spirit testifies to him of his pardon. When he thinks on Christ's empty tomb, the Holy Spirit testifies to him of his freedom. When he thinks on Christ's resurrection, the Holy Spirit testifies to him that he has been raised into the family of God.

But, be warned, if you are looking for feelings to convince you of your salvation, those feelings may never come. Why? Because if God gave you a peaceful feeling, and that feeling gave you assurance, then you would lose your assurance when the feeling went away. *Lasting* peace is found in the everlasting sacrifice of Jesus. God doesn't give us feelings to confirm His Word; He gives His Word to confirm our feelings. Rest in the Spirit's testimony of Jesus, which given in His Word.

Colossians 1:20 says Jesus, *"made peace through the blood of his cross . . ."* Peace is not what you feel; peace is what Jesus made through the blood of His cross. If you look for peace, therefore, you will never find it, but if you look to Jesus' cross, His peace will find you. In her book, "Messages of God's Abundance," Corrie Ten Boom said, "I looked to Jesus, and the dove of peace flew into my heart. I looked at the dove of peace; and lo . . . off it went."

19 THE UNPARDONABLE SIN

Wherefore I say unto you, All manner of sin and blasphemy shall be forgiven unto men: but the blasphemy [against] the [Holy] Ghost shall not be forgiven unto men. (Matthew 12:31)

Nothing is scarier than thinking you may have committed the unpardonable sin. When a person believes he's committed the unpardonable sin, he will experience the feeling of hopelessness, terror, and despair. If I had to choose one word to describe the feelings people have in this condition, it would be the word "torment."

In this chapter, I'm not going to explain away the warning Jesus gave in the above verse. That will not help you, and it will not honor Jesus. Rather, by God's grace, I would like to explain what Jesus said, so you can have a clear understanding of the passage and (by God's grace) receive the much-needed comfort you seek.

To understand the warning Jesus gave, we need to understand the occasion in which He gave it. In Matthew 12:22-32, we read:

> *Then was brought unto him one possessed with a devil, blind, and dumb: and he healed him, insomuch that the blind and dumb both spake and saw. And all the people were amazed, and said, Is not this the son of David? But when the Pharisees heard [it], they said, This [fellow] does not cast out devils, but by Beelzebub the prince of the devils. And Jesus knew their thoughts, and said unto them, Every kingdom divided against itself is brought to desolation; and every city or house divided against itself shall not stand: And if Satan cast out Satan, he is divided against himself; how shall then his*

kingdom stand? And if I by Beelzebub cast out devils, by whom do your children cast [them] out? therefore they shall be your judges. But if I cast out devils by the Spirit of God, then the kingdom of God is come unto you. Or else how can one enter into a strong man's house, and spoil his goods, except he first bind the strong man? and then he will spoil his house. He that is not with me is against me; and he that gathers not with me scatters abroad. Wherefore I say unto you, All manner of sin and blasphemy shall be forgiven unto men: but the blasphemy [against] the [Holy] Ghost shall not be forgiven unto men. And whosoever speaks a word against the Son of man, it shall be forgiven him: but whosoever speaks against the Holy Ghost, it shall not be forgiven him, neither in this world, neither in the [world] to come.

After healing this blind and dumb man, verse 23 says, "*And all the people were amazed, and said, Is not this the son of David?*" By calling Jesus the *"son of David,"* the people were saying Jesus was the King of kings—the King the Old Testament promised would descend from David's lineage to take His rightful place on the throne, destroy our enemies, and bring peace to the world.

Those who witnessed this miracle accurately noted the superior power Jesus exercised over the kingdom of the Devil, by casting this demon out of the blind and dumb man. Thus, they recognized that Jesus was their long-awaited King.

The blasphemers, on the other hand, denied that Jesus was the son of David. They saw the wonderful work the Holy Spirit had done. They saw how the Holy Spirit, through Jesus, had cast the devil out. But, though they saw what God's Spirit had done, they claimed the Devil did it. And Jesus called them out for speaking against the Holy Spirit in this way.

Jesus exposed their foolishness in verses 26 and 28: "*if Satan cast out Satan, he is divided against himself; how shall then his kingdom stand? . . . But if I cast out devils by the Spirit of God, then the kingdom of God is come unto you.*"

I see no need to be confused over these verses. Jesus was very clear when He described their sin. He said, "*whosoever speaks against the Holy Ghost, it shall not be forgiven him, neither in this world, neither in the world to come.*"

If you have not spoken against the Holy Spirit, then you have not committed this sin. Blasphemy is not unforgivable. Jesus said,

"All manner of sin and blasphemy shall be forgiven unto men. . ."

I believe the most enlightening passage in the Bible on this topic is the personal testimony of the apostle Paul, who, before he was saved, had blasphemed the work of Jesus Christ. But, Paul said his blasphemy was forgiven because he did it in ignorance.

In 1 Timothy 1:13, Paul said he *"was before a blasphemer, and a persecutor, and injurious."* Yet, Paul went on to say, *"but I obtained mercy, because I did it ignorantly in unbelief."*

When the apostle Paul spoke against Christ, threw Christians in jail, and approved of their murders, he was surely speaking and working against the work of the Holy Spirit. No doubt he thought the work of Christ was the work of the Devil. However, once he was enlightened by the Holy Spirit as to who Christ was, Paul quit speaking *against* Jesus and started speaking *for* Jesus. The two men who died on the cross next to Jesus also spoke against Jesus, but one later repented and Jesus saved him.

So, just because you've been a blasphemer, it doesn't mean you've committed the unpardonable sin. We must remember that these men *said* what they *said* after they *saw* what they *saw*. These men didn't make a careless statement one day during a theological discussion. And they didn't make this comment out of ignorance. No! They made this comment as eyewitnesses to a miracle of Jesus Christ.

My point is, the unpardonable sin we read about in Matthew 12 was not a sin of ignorance. If Paul would have blasphemed the work of Jesus after he saw Him (alive from the dead) on the road to Damascus, for example, then he could have no longer blasphemed in ignorance. If you have said something out of ignorance, therefore, then I believe you (like Paul) will receive mercy. For that matter, if you have said (or done) something that's made you wonder if you've committed the unpardonable sin, then you probably have not. For, if you had intended to blaspheme you surely would know it.

I once spoke to a person on the phone who, while under duress, purposefully spoke a word against the Holy Spirit. The Devil had harassed this man's mind, telling him over and over again to say something against the Holy Spirit. I mean, the Devil continued and continued until, finally, in order to gain some relief in his head, this poor person broke down and said something bad about the Holy Spirit. Of course, as soon as he did, what do you think the Devil did? He harassed this person more, this time telling him he should have never committed the unpardonable sin.

One moment the Devil was telling him to do it, and the next moment the Devil was telling him, "You shouldn't have done that!" This person was terrified and wanted to know if he had committed the unpardonable sin. He wanted me to let him know if he could be forgiven.

Perhaps you need to be forgiven for some terrible sin such as this. Whatever your case may be, you need to remember that we are saved through the work of the Holy Spirit. The Holy Spirit is the one who produces repentance and faith in our hearts. Jesus said the following in (John 16:7-14):

> *Nevertheless I tell you the truth; It is expedient for you that I go away: for if I go not away, the Comforter will not come unto you; but if I depart, I will send him unto you. And when he is come, he will reprove the world of sin, and of righteousness, and of judgment: Of sin, because they believe not on me; Of righteousness, because I go to my Father, and you see me no more; Of judgment, because the prince of this world is judged. I have yet many things to say unto you, but you cannot bear them now. Howbeit when he, the Spirit of truth, is come, he will guide you into all truth: for he shall not speak of himself; but whatsoever he shall hear, that shall he speak: and he will show you things to come. He shall glorify me: for he shall receive of mine, and shall show it unto you.*

The Holy Spirit is the one who convicts us of sin, warns us of judgment, and shows us the righteousness and salvation of Jesus Christ. The Holy Spirit is the one who guides us into the truth of the gospel and who glorifies and teaches us about Jesus. This means, apart from the Holy Spirit, you cannot appreciate, desire, or seek after the salvation of Jesus Christ. Apart from the Holy Spirit, you cannot (like Paul) repent of your blasphemy. The Bible says in Romans 2:4 that it is the goodness of God that leads us to repentance.

Therefore, if you are sorry for your sin, and if you are seeking salvation through the cross of Jesus Christ, then you can rest assured, God's Holy Spirit has not rejected you. If you want Jesus, it is because God wants you. Think about it: If you want to know and serve God through faith in the One who died for you, that's not the Devil pointing you to Jesus. Those desires come from the Spirit of God!

So, I am telling you on the authority of God's Word that, if you desire your sins to be forgiven through the death and shed blood of Jesus Christ, those holy desires are your surest proof that the Spirit of God is inviting you to do so.

The blasphemers in Matthew 12 opposed Christ's kingdom. But if you will bow the knee to King Jesus, and be a citizen of His kingdom, then an entrance therein surely awaits you.

Perhaps you are thinking right now, "If only I heard Jesus say what you just said, then I would know I can be saved." Well, that's great, because Jesus is the one who said it. Listen to His words in John 7:37-38, *"In the last day, that great day of the feast, Jesus stood and cried, saying, If any man thirst, let him come unto me, and drink. He that believes on me, as the scripture has said, out of his belly shall flow rivers of living water."*

Are you thirsting to be saved? Jesus said, if any man thirst, let him come. If you are thirsting for Jesus, it is the Holy Spirit who created that thirst. Just as physical thirst is a sure sign that there is a place for water in your body, so spiritual thirst is a sure sign that there is a place for Jesus in you. So drink! Drink the full promise of forgiveness offered to you in Jesus' death, and confidently quench your thirsty soul with the water of His cross.

20 DO I HAVE TO KNOW THE DAY I WAS SAVED?

And this is life eternal, that they might know you the only true God, and Jesus Christ, whom you have sent. (John 17:3)

On several occasions, I've heard preachers say, "If you don't know the day you were saved, then you are not saved." I remember hearing a radio preacher teach so passionately about this once. He said, "You can't tell me that you can meet a man like Jesus Christ and not remember the day you met Him!" Of course, he wasn't saying you have to know the calendar date when you were saved, but he was teaching that you must know the particular occasion or experience when you were saved.

Preachers like this teach that if you can't pinpoint the specific time of your conversion, then you were never saved. But there is only one problem with that statement: it's not in the Bible. The next time someone tells you that you have to know the day you were saved, I suggest you humbly ask him to show you where it says that in God's word. If he's sincere about his ministry, it may cause him to rethink what he said. But, if he's prideful, he will probably give you a song and dance, but he won't give you a Bible verse for what he's claimed, because there's not one.

As preachers, we must be very careful about what we say concerning a person's salvation. Making a provocative statement in church to get a quick "amen" is never worth the long-term harm we may cause someone by making bold, yet unbiblical, comments.

KNOWING I'M SAVED

While most people can point back to the specific time of their conversion, not everybody shares the same experience. For example, when I was a young man, I went through a long state of confusion about my salvation. I had heard so many things about being saved, many of which contradicted each other, and I wasn't sure what to believe.

Eventually, as the Lord began opening my eyes to the truth of the gospel, I did finally come to believe in Jesus alone for my salvation. But, because the Devil continued to confuse me on some of these issues, I continued to struggle a bit. During this period of time, therefore, there would be times when I trusted in Jesus. But, there were also times when I'd be troubled, and I would get confused again about the issue of faith and works. Or, I would wonder if my faith was genuine, etc.

Thankfully, I finally did settle in my understanding of the gospel, and I grew in my faith in Christ. But I am not sure when I was actually saved. Was it when I first began to believe in Christ? Was it sometime in the middle of my struggle? Or was it when I finally became settled in my faith and understanding?

Only God knows, so I will leave those things to Him. I just know I have Jesus, so I know I have eternal life. But, for a time, because of the statements I heard preachers make about having to know the day we are saved, I was greatly distressed. Eventually, thank God, I realized those preachers were wrong, as God showed me how their statements were not based on His Word.

Suppose you took a jet from Germany to Dallas, Texas. During your flight, you flew several hours and crossed many jurisdictional boundaries. When you landed at the Dallas airport, you were glad to be in Texas.

But suppose a flight attendant tells you that if you don't know the moment you crossed the Texas state line, then you are not in Texas. Not only would her statement be silly, but it could also be easily disproved. How? You'd know you were in Texas because you were standing in Texas. And, the fact that you were in Texas at that very moment was proof that you entered Texas at some time in the past.

The assurance of our salvation is not a matter of knowing *when* we believed in the past but knowing *who* we believe in the present. The apostle Paul knew the day he was saved, but, when he spoke of the confidence of his salvation, he didn't tell Timothy, "I know when I have believed . . ." He told Timothy, *"I know whom I have believed . . ."* (2 Timothy 1:12).

Jesus said in John 5:24, *"Truly, truly, I say to you, He that hears my word, and believes on him that sent me, has everlasting life . . ."* Have you heard the gospel and believe on Jesus as your Savior? If you do, then you have everlasting life! And, the fact that you believe in Him *today* is proof that you placed your faith in Him at some time in the *past*. So, believe on Him now, and never let present confidence be shaken by past confusion.

21 UNDERSTANDING REPENTANCE

Testifying both to the Jews, and also to the Greeks, repentance toward God, and faith toward our Lord Jesus Christ. (Acts 20:21)

In the above text, we see that the apostle Paul preached a gospel that consisted of two components: *repentance toward God,* and *faith toward our Lord Jesus Christ.* We generally hear a lot about faith toward Jesus, but we don't always hear so much about repentance toward God. So, in this chapter, I would like to explain to you what repentance is. To do this, I will use a text from the Old Testament. In Deuteronomy 20:10-13, God told Israel:

> *When you come near unto a city to fight against it, then proclaim peace unto it. And it shall be, if it makes you answer of peace, and open unto you, then it shall be, that all the people that are found therein shall be tributaries unto you, and they shall serve you. And if it will make no peace with you, but will make war against you, then you shalt besiege it: And when the Lord your God has delivered it into your hands, you shall smite every male thereof with the edge of the sword . . .*

This scripture passage is a marvelous illustration of how salvation works. But, to understand the illustration, you have to understand that the nation of Israel was the kingdom of God operating here on earth. As long as they were following God's commands, Israel was God's *servant* carrying out God's *will.*

When God began to form the nation of Israel, He caused Rebekah (Isaac's wife) to conceive Jacob. God later change Jacob's name to Israel, and Israel had twelve sons who became the twelve tribes of Israel. When Rebekah conceived Jacob, however, she noticed a lot of extra movement inside her womb. For, along with Jacob, there also came a non-identical twin brother named Esau.

And, even in the womb, those two little boys were already fighting over territory. In Genesis 25:22-23, we read, *"And the children struggled together within her . . . And the Lord said unto her, Two nations are in your womb, and two manner of people shall be separated from your bowels . . ."*

Did you catch that? God told Rebekah, *"Two nations are in your womb, and two manner of people . . ."*

Even as far back as Cain and Abel, the first two sons of Adam and Eve, we can see that in this world, there have always been two kinds of children—the children of *darkness* and the children of *light;* the children of *God's* kingdom and the children of the *Devil's* rebel kingdom. And, ever since sin entered into the world, these two nations (if you will) have been fighting over a territory called earth. God said this would happen in Genesis 3:15, *"And I will put enmity between you and the woman, and between your seed and her seed . . ."* In other words, her offspring and yours will always be enemies.

So, where does all this hostility and divisiveness come from? It comes from the rebellion of the Devil and those who follow him. For, although there are two kingdoms, there is only one King, and that King is God. Psalm 103:19, says, *"The Lord has prepared his throne in the heavens; and his kingdom rules over all."*

In time past, when God ruled as King in heaven, Lucifer, one of the angels God created, stirred up a number of other angels, encouraging them to turn against God and commit the unthinkable crime of anarchy. These rebellious angels were unthankful and unwilling to acknowledge the authority of their Creator, who had lovingly and marvelously made them. So, following the leadership of Lucifer, they conspired to overthrow the kingdom of God. Of course, nobody can fight against God and win, so their conspiracy was a failure.

When Lucifer (now called "the Devil") failed to overthrow God's kingdom, he was cast out of heaven down to earth, as Jesus described in Luke 10:18: *"I beheld Satan as lightning fall from heaven."* Unfortunately, the Devil's defeat didn't give him a change of heart. Instead, he figured if he couldn't rule in heaven, perhaps he could rule on earth. And that was the beginning of our problems.

When the Devil tempted Adam in the garden of Eden, he was trying to get Adam to commit a similar sin of anarchy on earth. By choosing to eat from one of the two trees in the garden of Eden, Adam would be choosing either *for* or *against* God's rule over his life. By eating from the Tree of Life, Adam would be accepting God's rule over him, and he would thus think and know everything that was good and right. But if Adam ate from the Tree of the Knowledge of Good and Evil, he would be rejecting God's rule over his life, and he would thus open his heart to know *evil*. This is what the Devil tempted Adam to do. And, yielding to the Devil's temptation, Adam chose self-rule—to know not only good but also evil.

If you ever wanted to know why Adam and Eve were not ashamed of their nakedness before they ate from this tree, it was because before they ate from the Tree of the Knowledge of *Good* and *Evil*, they could only know their bodies in a *good* way. But now, thanks to Adam's sinful choice, it seems people mostly know nakedness in a *bad* way. Likewise, thanks to Adam's choice, we can (and do) imagine all kinds of evil crimes to commit against our neighbors.

Sadly, most people in this world are like Adam. Following suit with the Devil, they live in a state of rebellion against their God and King. A person would have to be blind to not see how this world looks up to God and says, "Don't tell us what to do!" The world wants to keep God out of their government and out of their schools. Having rejected God as their King, the rebellious majority comprises what the Bible calls, *the kingdom of this world*—a kingdom whose capital city is no longer heaven.

But there are some people who don't agree with the rebellious majority. Like everybody else, these people (being born in sin) once belonged to the kingdom of this world. But, they were *called out* of this rebellious kingdom, and they were invited to join the kingdom of God. Today, the kingdom of God is known as the "church" (church means "called out"). But, in times past, the kingdom of God was known as the nation of Israel.

The church, therefore, is a group of people who recognize God as their King, and they recognize earth (God's creation) as a territory in His kingdom. Having acknowledged these evident truths, they submit themselves to the rule of God, their King.

When you think of the nation of Israel in the Old Testament, therefore, you must think of them as the kingdom of God operating on earth, because that is exactly what they were *called out of Egypt* to do.

Isaiah 44:6 says, *"Thus says the Lord the King of Israel, and his redeemer the Lord of hosts; I am the first, and I am the last; and beside me there is no God."*

Since Adam's rebellion, the kingdom of God and the kingdom of this world have always been in a state of conflict with one another, each struggling for their kingdom to rule here on the earth. So, when you read about the nation of Israel entering the Promised Land, overthrowing the cities therein, and capturing the land (like our verse in Deuteronomy), what you are really seeing is a picture of the kingdom of God executing judgment upon God's enemies and reclaiming territory that was once lost to rebel forces.

There is a great lesson to be learned by this. Namely, if you think an all-knowing, all-powerful God is going to allow a world He created to be lost to a bunch of two-bit rebels, you better think again. It may look bad now, but, before this is all over, the kingdom of God, to which the church belongs, will once again bare rule on this earth.

Psalm 47:2-3, says, *"For the Lord most high is terrible; he is a great King over all the earth. He shall subdue the people under us, and the nations under our feet."* Concerning this very thing, Jesus taught us to pray, in Matthew 6:10, *"Thy kingdom come. Thy will be done in earth, as it is in heaven."*

In his sermon, "The Witness of His coming", the late Dr. Adrian Rogers once said, "Rather than moaning, 'What's the world coming to?' start saying, 'Look Who's coming to the world. His name is Jesus.'"

King Jesus will be coming soon to take this world back. But the day He comes will be a dark and terrible day. Because, to take His kingdom back, He will have to drive the rebels out of it. He will have to destroy that rebel kingdom – those who never became citizens of God's kingdom by bowing their knee to King Jesus.

Speaking of those people and that day, Revelation 17:14 says, *"These shall make war with the Lamb, and the Lamb shall overcome them: for he is Lord of lords, and King of kings: and they that are with him are called, and chosen, and faithful."*

Yes, the King is coming, and He will overcome His enemies. But, I would like to tell you something great about our King. And it is this: He would rather save his enemies then slay them. Just listen to the marching orders King Jesus gave His army back in Deuteronomy 20:10 again. He said, *"When you come near unto a city to fight against it, then proclaim peace unto it."*

This is amazing. It shows you a great deal about the character of our God. He doesn't want to fight His creatures; He wants to save them. 2 Peter 3:9, says, *"The Lord is not slack concerning his promise, as some men count slackness; but is longsuffering to us-ward, not willing that any should perish, but that all should come to* [and here's our word] *repentance."*

By telling Israel to proclaim peace to the city, God was essentially saying, "I would rather them make peace with Me than I make war with them."

Let's look at Deuteronomy 20:11, *"And it shall be, if it make thee answer of peace, and open unto thee, then it shall be, that all the people that is found therein shall be tributaries unto thee, and they shall serve thee."*

God said if the people wanted to make peace, then this would be the provision for that peace: that nation would have to surrender their independence and become tributaries (servants) to God's kingdom and to God's people. Most people have a problem with that. I'm sure most of the cities Israel came against did not want to lose their independence and becoming tributaries to God's kingdom.

People love their independence. I like my independence, too. I believe in freedom. But there are some things I do not want to be independent of.

The last time I went to an amusement park, I rode one of those really fast roller coasters. Believe me, before that ride began, I wanted to make sure I was in bondage to my seat. Both I and the park staff checked my seatbelt and harness to make sure I was locked in real tight. When you're traveling sixty miles per hour upside down, it's not a good time to exercise your freedom. If you do, you will not only be *free*; you will also be a *casualty*.

No, I didn't want to be free from my seat; I wanted to be bound to my seat. Because as long as I was bound to my seat, I was free to enjoy the ride. In the same way, I don't want to be free from my God, because if I am in bondage to my God, then I am free to enjoy life without becoming a casualty of sin.

In Matthew 16:25, Jesus said, *"For whosoever will save his life shall lose it: and whosoever will lose his life for my sake shall find it."* By these cities giving up their independence to God, they were acknowledging the fact that God's kingdom had jurisdiction over their lives. And, acknowledging that, they abandoned self-rule and placed themselves under the rule of God's kingdom, becoming His tributaries.

A tributary is someone who acknowledges the authority of another nation. And he or she demonstrates subjection to that nation by paying tribute to his or her king—that is, by rendering a certain portion of their goods and services to him. By the way, that's what we do when we work and serve in the church. When we pass the offering plate, for example, we are paying tribute to our King.

Christians are people who understand they were born into a rebellious kingdom. But, because they acknowledge the authority of God's kingdom, they renounce their citizenship to the rebellious kingdom they were born in, and they pledge allegiance to King Jesus. This is what the Bible calls repentance.

Why is it necessary for us to have repentance toward God before we can have faith in Jesus as our Savior? Because you can never see yourself as a transgressor of God's laws unless you first acknowledge the authority He has over you. Some countries have laws that condemn Christians, but I do not acknowledge their authority over me, so I do not yield to their law.

Some people wrongly believe that repentance is a change of action. This is not true; any hypocrite can change his action. Repentance is not a change of *action*; repentance is a change of *mind*. Biblical repentance is not what you do; Biblical repentance is who you crown. Repentance is a change of mind that acknowledges the authority of God and the truth of the gospel.

Paul confirms this in Titus 1:1, *"Paul, a servant of God, and an apostle of Jesus Christ, according to the faith of God's elect, and the acknowledging of the truth . . ."*

Okay, let's get back to God's marching orders to Israel in Deuteronomy 20:12-13: *"And if it will make no peace with you, but will make war against you, then you shall besiege it: And when the Lord your God has delivered it into your hands, you shall smite every male thereof with the edge of the sword . . ."*

For those who would not repent and accept God's peace, the penalty was death. When the Israelites were preparing to fight against the city of Jericho, they came across a citizen of that city named Rahab. Though Rahab was a citizen of the city, she was a woman who acknowledged the authority of God over her life. In Joshua 2:10-11, she told the Israelites,

> *For we have heard how the Lord dried up the water of the Red sea for you, when ye came out of Egypt; and what you did unto the two kings of the Amorites, that were on the other side Jordan, Sihon and Og, whom you utterly destroyed. And as soon as we had heard these things, our hearts did melt, neither did there remain any more courage in any man, because of you: for the Lord your God, he is God in heaven above, and in earth beneath.*

Rahab knew God was about to judge her people, so she made peace with God before God made war with her. I believe the whole point of these verses in Deuteronomy is to show us that, before God came to make war with the people, He first gave the people an opportunity to make peace with Him. He said to the army of Israel, *"proclaim peace unto it."*

And, friend, that's exactly what God is doing with the gospel—He is proclaiming peace unto us.

In Luke 2:13-14, we read, *"And suddenly there was with the angel a multitude of the heavenly host praising God, and saying, Glory to God in the highest, and on earth peace, good will toward men."*

In Revelation 11:15, we read, *"And the seventh angel sounded; and there were great voices in heaven, saying, The kingdoms of this world are become the kingdoms of our Lord, and of his Christ; and he shall reign forever and ever."*

This means God is coming to overthrow this world and take His kingdom back. And He wants you to make peace with Him before He makes war with you. Have you made peace with the King? If not, why don't you acknowledge His authority over your life right now and accept the peace He made at the cross—the peace He's proclaiming to you in the gospel of Jesus Christ?

22 I CANNOT REPENT!

For godly sorrow works repentance to salvation not to be repented of: but the sorrow of the world works death. (2 Corinthians 7:10)

Perhaps you know you need to be saved, and you want to be saved, but you find it impossible to repent. Does it seem to you that the cross of Jesus has been set before your eyes, but a cold and unrepentant heart keeps it out of reach? Do you want to have "godly sorrow" but find it difficult to feel remorse for your sin?

If this describes you, then you don't have a *lack* of repentance; you have a *misunderstanding* of it. In the New Testament, when we see the word "repentance" used in connection with salvation, that word is translated from the Greek word *metanoia* (met-an'-oy-ah) or from a similar Greek word that has *metanoia* as its root word.

Metanoia is comprised of two smaller Greek words that have been put together to make one. The first part (meta) is a preposition that, when used alone, is most often translated as the word "after." The second part (noia) means to exercise the mind, to comprehend, to understand.

Metanoia: After + Exercise the Mind.

Here's what Jesus said in Matthew 21:28-29, *"A certain man had two sons; and he came to the first, and said, Son, go work to day in my vineyard. He answered and said, I will not: but afterward he repented, and went."*

The son, who first thought one way in his mind, afterward

thought differently about it. After he had time to think it over, he changed his mind and did what his father told him to do. In the same way, after we've considered our sin and the gospel of Jesus Christ, we acknowledge that we were wrong, and we receive the mercy of the cross before it's too late.

To repent, therefore, is to agree with the indictment God's law brings against you. Instead of making excuses for your sin, you plead guilty to the sins you've committed. Then, having pled guilty to your crimes (repent), you appeal your case to the cross (faith). That is how repentance and faith work together.

Isaiah 1:18 says, *"Come now, and let us reason together, says the Lord: though your sins be as scarlet, they shall be as white as snow . . ."* To repent is to be reasonable with God and own responsibility for your sin. While it's normal to feel sorry for your sin, however, it's not necessary to do so. The human mind is a complicated thing, and not everybody responds emotionally the same way.

2 Corinthians 7:10 says, *"godly sorrow works repentance to salvation . . ."* Because of this verse, many people believe they must feel "godly sorrow" in order to have repentance. And, if they don't feel that sorrow, they are afraid they cannot repent. But, in this verse, Paul is not trying to define repentance; he is trying to justify the sorrow he caused the Corinthians—the sorrow he caused when he rebuked them in his first letter. Proverbs 27:6 words it this way, *"Faithful are the wounds of a friend . . ."*

Misunderstanding Paul's words, some believe they must experience a feeling of "godly sorrow" before they can receive Christ. Some early American churches even had "mourners' benches" placed at the front of the church where people could weep and pray for their salvation. People like this, view repentance as an experience they must have when their heart is broken over sin, and when, in tearful remorse, they tell God they are sorry for all the wrong they've done. And only after they've "repented" of their sins in this way, do they believe they may proceed on to the next step and receive Christ as their Savior.

Don't misunderstand what I'm saying here. I'm not saying we should never feel sorry for our sins. It is both good and normal to experience sorrow for wrongdoing. But stronger emotions (like fear) can suppress our sense of sorrow, and the fatigue of spiritual battle can drain it dry. Do not fret over this.

Repentance is a motion of the mind, not an emotion of the

heart. We must make this distinction. For, some people will exercise their minds and agree with God about their sin (repentance), yet find it impossible to exercise their emotions and grieve over it.

They know they are sinners; they know they need Christ, and they truly want what He has done for them on the cross. But, when they come to the cross for salvation, they feel as if a cold breeze blows upon their hearts, and they can no more squeeze sorrow from their hearts than they could squeeze water from a rock.

Hence, they become sorrowful, frustrated, and afraid, because they cannot accomplish what they believe "repentance" is, and thus feel unqualified and incapable of believing in Jesus as their Savior. As odd as it sounds, they are actually sorry that they do not feel sorry (for their sins). They have sorrow because they do not have sorrow. Does this describe you? If it does, let me encourage you.

Consider Abel in the book of Genesis. He came to God by faith. He exercised his mind. He agreed with God that he was a sinner, and he knew God could only accept him on the basis of the Lamb of God who was promised to come.

So, Abel placed upon the altar the only hope he had, a spotless lamb that was slain—a picture of the Lamb to come (Jesus). Because of this, God accepted Abel. And if you will make Jesus the basis of your hope, God will accept you, too.

But, you say, "Must I not first grieve and lament over my sins?"

The answer is no. For, it is your sins that qualify you to believe in Christ, not your sorrow.

1 Timothy 1:15 says, *"This is a faithful saying, and worthy of all acceptation, that Christ Jesus came into the world to save sinners . . ."*

Sick people need a physician, not those who are well. So don't make the mistake of trying to get your heart well before coming to Christ. Shall you stitch up your wounds before coming to the Great Physician? Shall you wash and bandage them first? Not at all.

You must come to Jesus as you are. Come to Him as those in the Bible came to Him. Come to Him weak. Come to Him paralyzed. Come to Him sick, and sore, and utterly unclean, trusting that His blood and grace are sufficient to meet your needs.

Do not attempt to make yourself well. Do not attempt to get your sick heart in order. This is the work of the Physician. There is no work for you to do. Romans 4:5 says, *"But to him that works not, but believes on him that justifies the ungodly, his faith is counted for righteousness."*

Perhaps you have prayed for God to give you a broken heart so you could trust in Jesus. But God did not give you that broken heart. You are still numb inside, and you wonder why. God may not give you the feelings you desire, lest you rest a portion of your confidence in the remorse you feel, instead of in the blood Jesus shed.

The fact is, feelings are not worthy of your trust. If God gave you a feeling of sorrow right now, it would still not suffice you. For how would you know if your remorse was genuine? How would you know if your sorrow was intense enough? You wouldn't, and thus your hope of salvation would always come into question.

But if your faith rests on Christ alone, then nothing about you is ever brought into question, for your hope of salvation does not depend on what you did, or on how you feel, but it is based on what Jesus did for you, when He lived, died, and rose again in your place.

Don't be concerned with your lack of emotion. Come to God like Abel, laying nothing on your altar except the Lamb that died for you. Should we dare catch our tears in a bottle and lay them on the altar with Jesus? Need we hang a broken heart upon the cross for God to see? Shall these things improve what Christ has done? No. Summoning up feelings is not biblical repentance. In fact, it is more a sin of unbelief, for it disregards the full atonement and merit of Jesus Christ.

Do not offer God your sorrow. Offer Him your Savior. Just come to God as you are and trust completely in who Jesus is and in what Jesus has done for you. Come to Him, cold heart and all, not trusting that Jesus will make your heart acceptable, but trusting that God will accept you upon the basis of the perfect heart of Christ, which He offered to God on the cross as a substitute for yours.

Just as Toplady wrote in his hymn, Rock of Ages, come to Jesus and say...

Should my tears forever flow
Should my zeal no languor know
These for sin cannot atone
Thou must save and thou alone
Nothing in my hand I bring
Simply to thy cross I cling

23 DO I HAVE TO DO GOOD WORKS TO BE SAVED (OR STAY SAVED)?

Are we saved by faith, by works, or by a combination of both? Some people would say we are *saved* by our faith but *kept* by our works. Others would argue that we are saved (and kept) by faith alone.

The question of faith and works is something men have died for, and it is a matter of utmost importance. For how we understand the relationship of faith and works will determine whether we trust in what Jesus did for us or in what we do for Jesus. You see, it is really not a matter of faith or works; it is a matter of *Jesus* or *you*.

How we view our part in salvation directly affects how we view Christ's part in salvation. For example, did Jesus' death pay the penalty for *all* of our sins? Or was Jesus' death only a "down payment" for the penalty, and are we supposed to keep up the "monthly installments"? When we think of it this way, we can see how any demand for work on our part assumes a lack of work on His part.

I will not hesitate to answer this question for you: your salvation is *finished*, just like Jesus said. There is no clearer message in the Word of God than the message that *"Salvation belongs unto the Lord . . ."* (Psalm 3:8). So if you will be saved, it will be on the basis of Jesus' merit, not your own. There is only one way to heaven, and it's not by works; it's by grace through faith in the shed blood of Jesus Christ.

Romans 4:4 says, *"Now to him who works is the reward not reckoned of grace, but of debt."* In other words, if you could work for your salvation, then God would owe it (be indebted to give it) to you. But salvation is not something we earn; it is something we receive as a free gift (grace). So, in the very next verse the Bible says, *"But to him who works not, but believes on him who justifies the ungodly, his faith is counted for righteousness."*

Salvation is not given to the person who works for it. It is given to the person who *"works not,"* but *"believes"* on Jesus, who died in his place. Because of our faith in Jesus, the Bible says God justifies (pronounces innocent) the *"ungodly."* From start to finish, therefore, salvation is by the grace of God alone, apart from any good deeds we can do.

Most people get confused about faith and works because they don't understand the relationship between the Old and New Testaments. The Old and New Testaments are two covenants: the Covenant of the Law and the Covenant of Grace. Theoretically, if we could satisfy either of these two covenants, we would be viewed by God as sinless and would be accepted and free from condemnation. The Covenant of the Law and the Covenant of Grace are also known as, the Covenant of Moses and the Covenant of Christ. John 1:17 says, *"the law was given by Moses, but grace and truth came by Jesus Christ."*

In the above verse, notice how John makes a sharp contrast between these two covenants. This is because these covenants are not the same. The Covenant of the Law is satisfied by *works*; the Covenant of Grace is satisfied by *faith*. And you cannot mix these two covenants together. Like a fork in the highway, you can take one covenant or the other, but you cannot take both.

For a person to be accepted by God, he or she must make a choice between these two covenants and satisfy one of them completely (and exclusively). Under the covenant of the Law, you can attempt to enter heaven by how well you live. Under the covenant of Grace, you can choose to enter heaven by how well Jesus lived and died for you.

By their very nature, therefore, these two covenants mutually exclude one another. You can have grace or works, but you can't have both. Romans 11:6 says if salvation is *"by grace, then it is no more of works; otherwise grace is no more grace. But if it is of works, then it is no more of grace; otherwise work is no more work."*

Many people imagine salvation to be like a long race to heaven.

They think grace takes them the first part of the way, but they believe they must run the rest of the way on their own, while God cheers them on and picks them up from time to time. In other words, they believe their salvation begins with their faith but must be secured by their works. But the apostle Paul completely rejected this view, when he asked the Galatian church in Galatians 3:2-3, *"Did you receive the Spirit by the works of the law, or by the hearing of faith? Are you so foolish? having begun in the Spirit, are you now made perfect by the flesh?"*

Now that we know the difference between these two covenants, let's examine them together in greater detail. To do this, I would like for us to study the lives of two women in the Old Testament: Sarah and Hagar. Sarah and Hagar were real women in history. But, many years ago, God dipped His inspired brush into the circumstances of their lives and, by recording their stories, painted a marvelous picture for us of the salvation of Jesus Christ. Listen to the story of these two mothers, as we read several passages in the book of Genesis.

Genesis 11:29-30 says *"Abram's wife was Sarai . . . But Sarai was barren; she had no child."* Notice that Sarai, whose name was later changed to Sarah, had no child. Nevertheless, in the next chapter, God promised to bless her husband Abram with so many children that he would become a great nation. Because of this promise, God changed Abram's name to Abraham (Father of many nations).

In Genesis 15:5, God told Abraham, *"Look now toward heaven, and number the stars, if you be able to number them: and he said unto him, So shall your offspring be."* And, in verse 6, we are told Abraham *"believed in the Lord; and he counted it to him for righteousness."*

But Abraham and Sarah were very old. So Sarah, figuring she was too old to have a baby, thought Abraham should have a child through Hagar, her young Egyptian bondservant. Without consulting God first, Abraham agreed and went along with Sarah's plan. Genesis 16:1-2:

> *Now Sarai Abram's wife bore him no children: and she had an handmaid, an Egyptian, whose name was Hagar. And Sarai said to Abram, Behold now, the Lord has restrained me from bearing: I pray you, go in to my maid; it may be that I may obtain children by her. And Abram listened to the voice of Sarai.*

When Hagar conceived, she bore Abraham a son named Ishmael. But the nation God promised Abraham was not supposed to descend through Hagar's son, but through Sarah's son, by the grace of God. So, God kept His promise and gave Abraham a son through Sarah in their old age. Genesis 21:2-3 says, *"For Sarah conceived, and bore Abraham a son in his old age . . . And Abraham called the name of his son . . . whom Sarah bore to him, Isaac."*

As Isaac grew up, conflict developed between Isaac (Sarah's son) and Ishmael (the son of the bondwoman Hagar). Because of this conflict, the bondwoman and her son were cast out, and Isaac became the only heir to Abraham's estate. What we have to understand is, these two mothers (Sarah and Hagar) are Old Testaments illustrations of the two covenants of Law and Grace. Galatians 4:22-24 says, *"Abraham had two sons, the one by a bondmaid, the other by a freewoman . . . Which things are an allegory: for these are the two covenants . . ."*

Once again, there are only two covenants by which man can be accepted by God: Law and Grace. The Covenant of the Law is a mandate based on our performance; the Covenant of Grace is a gift based on Christ's performance. Let's see how this works.

Here is an example of the Covenant of the Law. It is found in Luke 10:25-28:

> *And, behold, a certain lawyer stood up, and tempted him, saying, Master, what shall I do to inherit eternal life? He said unto him, What is written in the law? How do you read it? And he answering said, You shall love the Lord your God with all your heart, and with all your soul, and with all your strength, and with all your mind; and your neighbor as yourself. And he said unto him, You have answered right: this do, and you shall live.*

To the man who sought to earn eternal life by obeying the Law, Jesus said, *"this do, and you shall live."* The Covenant of Grace, on the other hand, does not require us to work under the law. We read in Ephesians 2:8-9, *"For by grace are you saved through faith; and that not of yourselves:* [it is] *the gift of God: Not of works . . ."*

So, the Law says to us, "Do my will, and you shall live," but Grace says to Jesus, "Do my will, and man shall live." Do you see the difference?

Hagar was a *bondmaid*, so she represents the Covenant of the

Law, which God gave to Israel on Mt. Sinai. Since we all break the Law, this covenant keeps us in *bondage* to sin and death. Galatians 4:24 says, *". . .these women are two covenants; one from mount Sinai, bearing children unto bondage, which is Hagar."*

Sarah, on the other hand, was a free woman. She represents the Covenant of Grace, by which Jesus sets us free from our bondage to sin and death. Galatians 4:22 says, *"Abraham had two sons, the one by a bondmaid, the other by a freewoman."*

Like the sons of Hagar and Sarah, people born under the Law are born into bondage, but people born again by Grace are born into freedom. The Law imprisons us on account of our sin. Grace frees us on account of Jesus' righteousness.

Sarah was Abraham's original wife. Hagar only became Abraham's wife (concubine) because Sarah thought God might give Abraham a son through her handmaid. But Sarah was wrong. God had planned to give Abraham a son through Sarah from the very beginning. In the same way, God planned to save us by grace from the very beginning. The New Covenant of Grace was God's original covenant for salvation. We only call it the "New" Testament (Covenant) because, like Sarah's failed attempt to fulfill God's promise through Hagar, the Covenant of Grace wasn't revealed to us until after we failed to fulfill God's will by obeying the Old Testament Law.

In Titus 1:2 were are told that, before the world began, God promised to give us eternal life through the redemption of Jesus Christ (Grace). Regarding this truth, Spurgeon said, *". . . long ere seers preached the law, and long ere Sinai smoked. Long before Adam stood in the garden, God had ordained his people to eternal life that they might be saved through Jesus."*

Hagar was Sarah's handmaid. Likewise, the Law is the handmaid for Grace. The Law was given first to show us our sin, and it was only supposed to last until Jesus (the promised Son) came to die for that sin, just as Galatians 3:19 says, *"What purpose does the law serve? It was added because of transgressions, until the Seed* [the promised Son (Jesus)] *should come to whom the promise was made . . ."*

Hagar was never intended to give children to Abraham. So, when she was used for something she was not designed for, her son was cast out with no inheritance. In the same way, the Law was never intended to make us children of God. It was only meant to be a handmaid to Grace, by showing us our sins, and thus our need to be saved through Jesus' sacrifice.

Hagar was never free, and Sarah was never in bondage. In the same way, the Law will never free a man from sin, and Grace will never condemn a man who trusts in Jesus.

Now let's consider the two sons: Ishmael and Isaac. Ishmael was born first to the bondwoman Hagar. So, we are all born first into the Covenant (and curse) of the Law. Galatians 3:10 says, *"For as many as are of the works of the law, are under the curse: for it is written, Cursed is every one that continues not in all things which are written in the book of the law to do them."* This is why Jesus said in John 3:3, *"Except a man be born again* [a second birth], *he cannot see the kingdom of God."*

Ishmael was born by human performance, thus he is an illustration of man's unsuccessful attempt to gain eternal life by his own performance (works). Isaac, however, was born by the work of God, who gave life to a dead womb. Speaking of Abraham, Romans 4:19 says, *"being not weak in faith, he considered not his own body now dead, when he was about an hundred years old, neither yet the deadness of Sara's womb . . ."*

As God waited until Abraham and Sarah realized the "deadness" of their ability to have a son, so God waits until we realize the deadness of our own soul—that is, our utter inability to keep the Law, before He gives us Jesus. Ephesians 2:4-5 says, *"But God, who is rich in mercy, for his great love wherewith he loved us, Even when we were dead in sins, has made us alive together with Christ, (by grace you are saved;)."*

Isaac was born by God's promise, not by man's performance. And Galatians 3:18 says, *"if the inheritance is by the law, it is no more by promise: but God gave it to Abraham by promise."*

Ishmael mocked Isaac, as recorded in Genesis 21:8-9: *"And the child grew, and was weaned: and Abraham made a great feast the [same] day that Isaac was weaned. And Sarah saw the son of Hagar the Egyptian, which she had born unto Abraham, mocking."* Even so, the children of the Law still mock the children of Grace today. They say, "You people think you can sin all you want to and still be saved." Well, they are wrong: we don't want to sin. We don't come to Christ with a love for sin; we come to Him with a hatred for sin but with a need for grace.

Now that we have talked about the two covenants, let's consider the two destinations we face: heaven or hell. Only Isaac received the inheritance. Genesis 25:5-6 says, *"And Abraham gave all that he had unto Isaac. But unto the sons of the concubines, which Abraham had, Abraham gave gifts, and sent them away from Isaac his son . . .*" Those who come by Grace are joint heirs with Christ. Like Isaac, only they will receive the inheritance of eternal life from God their Father. But those who are not born of "Sarah"—those who are not saved by Grace, but who have tried to do their best according to the Law, they will be sent away.

We are told in Genesis 21:10 that *"Sarah . . . said unto Abraham, Cast out this bondwoman and her son: for the son of this bondwoman shall not be heir with my son,* [even] *with Isaac."* Likewise, in Matthew 8:12, Jesus said those who do not accept the New Testament, *"shall be cast out into outer darkness: there shall be weeping and gnashing of teeth."*

So here is our conclusion. There are two mothers: Sarah and Hagar; there are two covenants: Law and Grace; there are two sons: Ishmael and Isaac; and there are only two choices for you: Life or Death . . . Sarah or Hagar . . . Law or Grace . . . you or Jesus.

You will either gain eternal life by having your own righteousness (obeying the law and not sinning), or you will gain it by having Jesus' righteousness (trusting in Him who obeyed the Law on your behalf and died for your sin). Since we all have sinned, this leaves us only one choice: the grace of Jesus Christ.

In Galatians 2:21, the Holy Spirit gave us one of the most powerful statements in the Bible, when He, through the apostle Paul, said, *"I do not make void the grace of God: for if righteousness comes by the law, then Christ is dead in vain."*

24 WHAT IF I HAVE REJECTED JESUS BEFORE? CAN I STILL BE SAVED?

There are some who believe they are disqualified from receiving Jesus as their Savior because they didn't accept His salvation at some time in the past. Like the rich man who had died in Jesus' parable, they feel they can only stare into heaven but cannot go there. If you are one of these people, then the story of Joseph is for you.

If you are not familiar with the story of Joseph, I would like to encourage you to read it after you've read this paragraph (Genesis 42:1-45:7). Joseph was a rich man who was rejected by his brothers and sold as a slave in Egypt. Once Joseph was in Egypt, however, God caused a series of events to occur that resulted in Joseph being promoted from a slave to second in command over the whole kingdom. During Joseph's command, God had him prepare for a famine by storing up an abundance of grain. Then, when the famine came, Joseph's brothers had to buy bread from Joseph—the one they betrayed—or face starving to death.

The reason the story of Joseph should be important to you is because the rejection of Joseph is an Old Testament picture of man's rejection of Jesus Christ. Like Joseph, Jesus was rejected by His brethren (the Jews). But, also like Joseph, Jesus was raised up to be our King, and every person will one day bow the knee to Him. Genesis 42:6 says, *"And Joseph was the governor over the land, and he it was that sold to all the people of the land: and Joseph's brethren came, and bowed down themselves before him with their faces to the earth."*

Notice in the above verse that everybody had to go to Joseph to get bread: *"he it was that sold to all the people . . ."* Everyone has to eat to live. If people wanted bread during this famine, they had to go to Joseph to get it. This was a picture of the Lord Jesus, to whom we all must go for "bread" lest we die in our sins. In John 6:51, Jesus said, *"I am the living bread which came down from heaven: if any man eat of this bread, he shall live for ever: and the bread that I will give is my flesh, which I will give for the life of the world."*

If we want to eat "bread" that will make us live forever, then we have to go to Jesus to get it, for He gives bread to *"all the people of the land . . ."* During the famine in Egypt, getting bread to live was simple: People needed bread to live, and Joseph had bread to give. So they went to Joseph and got bread.

But getting bread was more difficult for Joseph's brothers. Like many church kids who grow up knowing about Jesus, but are not saved until much later in life, Joseph's brothers *knew* Joseph before they *appreciated* Joseph and realized their need for his bread. Before they got bread from Joseph, Joseph's brothers denied him, mistreated him, and outright rejected him, like many have done to Jesus.

When they were young, everything they heard about Joseph being their ruler was getting in the way of their plans. So, *"his brethren said to him, Shall you indeed reign over us? or shall you indeed have dominion over us? And they hated him yet the more . . ."* (Genesis 37:8).

They thought if Joseph became lord over them, it would surely hold them back in life. And, sadly, that's how many people who've grown up in church felt about Jesus. For this reason, people who've never heard the name of Jesus may find it easier to take "bread" from Him. Like the Egyptians who weren't raised up with Joseph, they know they need bread to live, and since Jesus has bread to give, they simply take His bread and live.

Perhaps you are like Joseph's brothers. Perhaps you knew Jesus before you realized your need for His "bread" of life. Like Joseph's brothers, you knew Jesus, but you failed to appreciate Him; you failed to accept Him. Ultimately, you denied Him, mistreated Him, and outright rejected Him.

Like Joseph's brothers, having Jesus as your Lord would have gotten in the way of all your plans. So, in your heart, you said to Jesus, *shall you indeed reign over me?* You entered life without the Christ you were introduced to as a child, and you rejected the influence of your godly parents.

But, like Joseph's brothers, you now face a time of great hunger in your life. And you want to go to Jesus for bread, because you want to live. But, like Joseph's brothers, you find it difficult to face the King you once rejected.

Like Joseph's brothers, perhaps your motives for coming to Christ are being questioned. Perhaps your heart accuses you of being insincere, a hypocrite, undeserving, unwelcome, and unwanted in the kingdom of God. It's okay. This is how Joseph's brothers felt, too.

Listen to how the Bible describes their experience in Genesis 42:9-15:

> *And Joseph remembered the dreams which he dreamed of them, and said unto them, You are spies; to see the nakedness of the land you are come. And they said unto him, No, my lord, but to buy food are your servants come. We are all one man's sons; we are true men, your servants are no spies. And he said unto them, No, but to see the nakedness of the land you are come. And they said, Your servants are twelve brethren, the sons of one man in the land of Canaan; and, behold, the youngest is this day with our father, and one is not. And Joseph said unto them, That is it that I spake unto you, saying, You are spies: Hereby you shall be proved . . .*

Do you see how their motives for coming to Joseph were questioned? Like Joseph's brothers, you may say to yourself, "I don't know if my motives are right. I'm not sure Jesus will accept me now."

Does this describe you? If it does, then let God's Word encourage you. Think about it: what did God use to bring those men to Joseph? He used hunger. These men didn't come with a *love* for Joseph; they came with a *hunger* for bread. All they knew was that if they didn't get bread from Joseph, they would die. And, like those men, if you don't get bread from Jesus, you will die. Make no mistake about it: bread is made for hungry people. So, if you want the Bread of Life, you can have Him!

If you are hungry for Jesus' bread, then (like Joseph's brothers) you should acknowledge your sin immediately and take that bread at once, just as Genesis 42:21 describes: *"And they said one to another, We are verily guilty concerning our brother, in that we saw the anguish of his soul, when he besought us, and we would not hear; therefore is this distress come upon us."*

I have dealt with so many people, who, because they once denied Jesus, are afraid He won't accept them. Like Joseph's brothers, they can point back to a specific time when Jesus was working in their lives, but they refused Him. Like Joseph's brothers, they sold Jesus out for a few pieces of earthly silver. But that silver has become worthless to them now, and they wish to exchange it for living bread.

Like Joseph's brothers, you may not realize Jesus still loves you. Don't be troubled. Jesus cares for you, and He understands what you are going through. Genesis 42:23 points this out: *"And they knew not that Joseph understood them . . ."* And Genesis 45:3 reiterates it: *"they were troubled at his presence."*

If you will go to Jesus, He will most certainly accept you. For Jesus said in John 6:37, *"him that comes to me I will in no way cast out."* If you wonder if you can still come to Jesus, here's your answer, found in Genesis 45:4: *"And Joseph said unto his brethren, Come near to me, I pray you. And they came near. And he said, I am Joseph your brother, whom you sold into Egypt."*

As it was with *Joseph*, so it is with *Jesus*. In spite of being rejected by these men, Joseph forgave them, received them, and lovingly said to them, *"Now therefore be not grieved, nor angry with yourselves, that you sold me here . . ."* (Genesis 45:5).

The Lord Jesus went to the cross because we (the human race) sold our Master out. We rejected the Lordship of our God. But when we go to the cross to receive the Bread of Life, it's as though Jesus lovingly says to us, *"be not grieved, nor angry with yourselves, that you sold me here . . ."*

Joseph's forgiveness was based on Joseph's purpose to give life, as articulated in Genesis 45:5 when he said, *"Now therefore be not grieved, nor angry with yourselves, that you sold me here: for God did send me before you to preserve life."* As God sent Joseph into Egypt that they might live, so God sent Jesus into the world that you might live. 1 John 4:9 says, *"In this was manifested the love of God toward us, because that God sent his only begotten Son into the world, that we might live through him."*

Like Joseph, God sent Jesus to save the world through His rejection. As Joseph's betrayal brought him into a position to save the world, so Jesus' betrayal brought Him to the cross to save me and you. God delivered the people He knew would betray Joseph, and, if you will come to Jesus, God will deliver you, too. Take this verse to heart in 1 Timothy 1:15: *"This is a faithful saying, and worthy of all acceptation, that Christ Jesus came into the world to save sinners . . ."*

If you're like Joseph's brothers and are afraid you can no longer be saved because you've rejected Jesus, then rest assured, Jesus is reaching out to you right now, saying, *"be not grieved, nor angry with yourselves . . ."* Come to Him now. You need bread to live, and Jesus has bread to give.

25 DO I HAVE TO BE BAPTIZED TO BE SAVED?

He that believes and is baptized shall be saved; but he that believes not shall be damned. (Mark 16:16)

The question of whether or not a person must be baptized in water to be saved is a highly contested topic. It has caused much division in the church. But it can cause confusion and doubt for Christians too.

Suppose a woman has been baptized, but she wonders if her baptism was performed properly. Maybe she should have been immersed instead of sprinkled. Maybe she was baptized by the wrong church. Whatever the situation may be, she wonders if God considers her baptism to be genuine. And, if not, she wonders if she must be re-baptized to go to heaven.

In this chapter, I pray the Holy Spirit will take the Word of God and clear up any confusion you may have about the role of water baptism in your salvation. Those who teach that one must be baptized in water to be saved only have a few verses in the Bible that appear to support their claim. Instead of commenting on every verse, I will show you one of these verses and then explain the true meaning of baptism. By doing this, I believe we can keep it simple and explain most of the other verses at the same time. In Mark 16:16, Jesus said, *"He that believes and is baptized shall be saved; but he that believes not shall be damned."*

In the first part of this verse, Jesus clearly said whoever believes and is baptized shall be saved, causing some to assume that we must both believe in Christ and be baptized in water to be saved. But in the latter part of the verse, Jesus only said, *"he that believes not shall be damned."* He did *not* say, *"he that is baptized not shall be damned."*

In fact, you will not find one scripture in the Bible where God says a person will be condemned if he is not baptized in water. You will find repeated warnings to those who do not believe, but you will never find a warning regarding baptism. And if God required water baptism for salvation, don't you believe He would warn us of the danger of not being baptized (or baptized correctly)?

So, if water baptism is not required for salvation, why did Jesus mention baptism in the verse we just read? And where did water baptism come from in the first place? What's it all about?

The New Testament concept of water baptism is based on the Old Testament washings that God commanded to be done with water. An example of this can be found in Leviticus 16:24, where God said the high priest *"shall wash his flesh with water in the holy place. . ."* In both the Old and New Testaments, these ceremonial washings represent Jesus washing our sins away, not by water, but by the sacrifice He made on the cross.

Revelation 1:5 tells us that Jesus *"loved us, and washed us from our sins in his own blood . . ."* When we put our faith in God's word concerning Jesus' death on the cross, our sins are "washed away". This is described for us in Ephesians 5:25-26, which tells us *"Christ . . .loved the church, and gave himself for it; (26) That he might sanctify and cleanse it with the washing of water by the word . . ."* This is the baptism that saves us, and it is the baptism of Jesus Christ.

The word "baptize" means to immerse and make fully wet. And it was first mentioned in connection with John the Baptist. Speaking of John the Baptist, the Apostle John said, in John 1:6-7, *"There was a man sent from God, whose name was John. The same came for a witness, to bear witness of the Light, that all men through him might believe."*

So, John the Baptist's ministry was less about baptizing people in water and more about getting them to believe in Jesus Christ. In fact, the whole idea behind John's baptism in water was to illustrate man's need to repent and believe in Jesus, who alone could wash away their sins.

The apostle Paul explained this in Acts 19:4, when he said, *"John verily baptized with the baptism of repentance, saying unto the people, that they should believe on him which should come after him, that is, on Christ Jesus."* John the Baptist himself said in John 3:36, *"He that believes on the Son has everlasting life . . ."*

Make no mistake about it: we are saved by placing our faith in Jesus, not by placing ourselves in water. John, therefore, baptized people in water, not to wash their sins away, but to make Jesus (the only one who can wash sins away) known to the world. John the Baptist said, in John 1:31, *"that he [Jesus] should be made manifest to Israel, therefore am I come baptizing with water."* The baptism that saves us, then, is not the washing that we receive from men, but the washing that we receive from Jesus Christ.

When God created Adam, God *"breathed into his nostrils the breath of life; and man became a living soul"* (Genesis 2:7). This "breath of life" is not simply talking about *respiration*; it is talking about *inspiration*. Adam was God's first temple. When God created Adam, God breathed His Spirit into Adam, and Adam was *inspired* (breathed into). But when Adam sinned, God's Spirit moved out of Adam, and Adam no longer experienced inspiration; he experienced *expiration* (death), because God's eternal life went out.

I said all of that to say this: The objective of salvation is not to get you out of earth and into heaven, but to wash away your sins and get the God of heaven back into you. This is what God prophesied He would do for us in the Old Testament, and this is what the baptism (washing) of Jesus Christ is all about. Look at this amazing prophecy in Ezekiel 36:25-27:

> *And I will sprinkle clean waters on you, and you shall be clean. I will cleanse you from all your filthiness and from your idols. (26) And I will give you a new heart, and I will put a new spirit within you. And I will take away the stony heart out of your flesh, and I will give you a heart of flesh. (27) And I will put My Spirit within you and cause you to walk in My statutes, and you shall keep My judgments and do them.*

When a person in the New Testament believes in Jesus as their Savior, the Holy Spirit of God enters into that person. That's why the apostle Paul said, in 1 Corinthians 3:16, *"Know you not that you are the temple of God, and that the Spirit of God dwells in you?"* So, once again, Jesus' baptism (salvation) removes our sins and makes us one with God. In John 17:21, Jesus prayed that all who believe in Him *"may be one; as you, Father, are in me, and I in you, that they also may be one in us . . ."*

The baptism of Jesus Christ and the baptism of the Holy Spirit are one and the same. The baptism of the Holy Spirit is not when a person speaks in tongues; the baptism of the Holy Spirit is when God washes away our sins by uniting us forever to the death, burial, and resurrection of Jesus Christ.

Simply put, therefore, the baptism that saves us is not the baptism of *water*, but the baptism of the *Holy Spirit*, who unites us to Jesus when we believe on him concerning the gospel message. The Bible says this in 1 Corinthians 12:13, *"For by one Spirit are we all baptized into one body, whether we be Jews or Gentiles, whether we be bond or free; and have been all made to drink into one Spirit."*

So, the baptism of John with water was only an illustration of the baptism of Jesus with the Spirit of God. John the Baptist said, in Mark 1:8, *"I indeed have baptized you with water: but he shall baptize you with the Holy Ghost."* That's no different than an Old Testament priest saying, "I indeed offer the sacrifice of animals: but He shall offer the sacrifice of Himself."

To be saved, you do not need the baptism of water that's administered by man; you need the baptism of the Spirit that's administered by Jesus. And this baptism is given to everyone the moment they believe the gospel message and trust Jesus as their Savior. Ephesians 1:13 says, *"In whom you also trusted, after that you heard the word of truth, the gospel of your salvation: in whom also after that you believed, you were sealed with that holy Spirit of promise . . ."*

Okay, if we don't have to be baptized in water to be saved, why do we still baptize people with water today? Water baptism symbolizes the Holy Spirit washing away our sins by uniting us to the death, burial, and resurrection of Jesus. As such, it is a beautiful way for us to demonstrate on the outside what we are trusting in on the inside.

Speaking of our baptism by the Holy Spirit, the apostle Paul explained in Romans 6:3-4:

> *Do you not know that as many of us as were baptized into Jesus Christ were baptized into His death? Therefore we were buried with Him by baptism into death, so that as Christ was raised up from the dead by the glory of the Father; even so we also should walk in newness of life.*

But speaking of our baptism by men in water, the Apostle Paul said in 1 Corinthians 1:14-17:

> *I thank God that I baptized none of you, but Crispus and Gaius; Lest any should say that I had baptized in mine own name. And I baptized also the household of Stephanas: besides, I know not whether I baptized any other. For Christ sent me not to baptize, but to preach the gospel...*

Did you catch that? Paul said, *"Christ sent me not to baptize, but to preach the gospel..."* Surely, if water baptism was necessary for salvation, then Paul could have never made a comment like that. Rather, he would have been baptizing as many people as he could. But Paul knew that water baptism had no power to save, which is why he said this in Romans 1:16, *"For I am not ashamed of the gospel of Christ, for it is the power of God unto salvation to everyone who believes..."*

Over the years, I have seen several instances in the news where, for one reason or another, somebody will put on a uniform and pretend to be a police officer. Many of those people will make traffic stops. Some will even use the uniforms to commit crimes. But, regardless of their motive, putting on a police uniform does not make these imposters officers of the law; it only deceives people for a time.

In 1989, I was commissioned as a state trooper, and I was issued my uniform. When I was off duty, I knew I was a police officer on the inside. But when I put on my uniform, the world saw I was a police officer on the outside. The uniform didn't make me an officer, but it made the fact that I was an officer known to those around me. In the same way, water baptism doesn't make us Christians; it just makes our Christianity known to those around us.

So don't put your faith in the water; put your faith in Jesus, and never let the issue of water baptism cause you to doubt your salvation again.

26 I STRUGGLE TO BELIEVE!

During times of intense spiritual warfare, it may seem like you must fight for the very existence of your faith. Even a strong Christian will sometimes find that the old Adam in him still wants to rise up and destroy (if it were possible) the work of faith the Holy Spirit has placed in his heart. Like an uninvited guest, evil thoughts and doubts about God will enter your mind, making you wonder if you truly believe.

You may know the experience I'm describing. One moment, you will be doing just fine. But the next thing you know, the Devil whispers into your ear, and says, "What if God's not real? What if Jesus is just a fairytale? What if you don't really believe?"

Immediately, you will come to your own defense and try to silence those doubts. You will battle them until you finally feel like your faith is back on solid ground. But the Devil is a clever strategist. He has plenty of time to wait, and he likes to be a step or two ahead of his opponents.

Already anticipating your move, the Devil now whispers into your other ear and says, "How terrible! You just doubted God! You doubted the Lord Jesus! You know what that means, don't you? That means you don't believe, or your faith in Jesus lapsed for a time."

The same Devil that put the doubt in your mind now accuses you of not being a true Christian, because (according to him) your faith is not consistent enough. To support his claim, the Devil will trouble you with a scripture such as Hebrews 3:14, *"For we are made partakers of Christ, if we hold the beginning of our confidence stedfast unto the end . . ."* If you will let him, the Devil will convince you that you are not a true believer. He will tell you that a true believer would never doubt like that, and that your lapse of faith is evidence that you are not saved. Does this sound familiar to you?

When it comes to the assurance of your salvation, never seek assurance in anything you do on a given day. We are inconsistent and unreliable creatures. Therefore, if we seek assurance based on what we think, how we feel, or how well we live (whether good or bad), we will always have an inconsistent and unreliable assurance.

For example, I may trust Jesus today, but I may have trusted Him better last week. So, how could I know if my faith in Jesus is enough? Since we are inconsistent creatures, you may be closer to Jesus today than you are tomorrow. This is why the gospel never points you to what you do on a given day, but to what Jesus did, when He died for you on the cross.

What Jesus did when He died and rose again, is a perfect, finished, and unchanging work. Thus, if you rely on that, you will have a perfect, finished, and unchanging assurance of your salvation. Although you waver and are inconsistent, Jesus never is. The blood He shed to pay the penalty for your sins has forever blotted out the debt you owe. So, don't put your faith in your faith or in yourself; put your faith in Him.

Suppose a person hears the gospel and rests his faith on the sacrifice Jesus made. Eventually, the Devil attempts to make the new believer doubt his salvation. So, seeking assurance, the believer runs back to the cross and clings to it as a drowning man would cling to a floating object.

Initially, this helps. But the believer finds himself running back to the cross over and over again as the Devil continues to harass him. After a while, the believer will grow weary with all this running and clinging.

If this cycle of faith and doubt continues, the new Christian will begin to see his faith as an effort he must continue, rather than seeing the cross as an accomplishment he can enjoy. Don't let the Devil trick you. He wants you to hang on to the cross as a man dangling from a cliff would hang on to a piece of rock. But Jesus paying the penalty for your sins is not an object for you to hang from; it is a fact for you to stand on and enjoy.

People who focus on their faith will sometimes feel the need to constantly exert their faith, even to the point of exhaustion. They may feel the need to continually be aware of the fact that they believe in Jesus, or to continually remind themselves (and God) that they believe. How wearisome this is! This may sound odd if you have never experienced this. But if you have, then you know exactly what I'm talking about.

Remember, faith has neither ability nor strength. Faith relies upon the ability and strength of something else. This is why God chose faith as the means for us to be saved. God ordained salvation to be by faith, so that we, who have no ability or strength in ourselves, could rely entirely on Jesus. But, failing to understand this, we will sometimes look to our faith when we should be looking to Him.

God isn't as concerned with your faith as He is concerned with what your faith is in. God is no more interested in your faith than He was interested in the little hyssop bush the Israelites used to apply blood to their doorposts on Passover night. The hyssop was only used to transport the blood to their door. After that, the little plant was probably thrown away and never thought of again.

God did not look at the hyssop that night; He looked at the blood. He said, ". . . when I see the blood, I will pass over you" (Exodus 12:3). In the same way, God only looks at the blood Jesus shed for you, and that's where you must look too. Just accept the blood of Christ as the payment for your sin, and think no more of the little hyssop shrub of faith.

On Passover, once they put the blood on their door, they rested confidently inside their home. They did not stand guard over the door with a hyssop bush and a bucket of blood in their hand, fearing an enemy might sneak over during the night and wash the blood away. And they didn't keep putting fresh coats of blood on the door to make it more visible for God to see. They just got behind the blood of the one that died for them, and that was the end of it.

Let's make this simple. Will you have Jesus as your Savior? Will you accept the blood He shed as the payment for your sin? If your answer is yes (and I believe it is), then you are saved. God knows the decision you've made concerning Jesus, and He will not forget it. Sure, your faith is not perfect. In fact, there is nothing about you that is perfect. But Jesus came to represent you perfectly to God. So you don't need a perfect faith; you just need a perfect Jesus.

Remember the serpent we mentioned in Chapter 13? There were an estimated two million Jews in the wilderness when God told them to look at that serpent. I'm sure the people who were far away must have had a very poor view of it. And some people, I am sure, were old and had poor vision. But God did not tell them to look *well*; God just told them to *look*.

It does not matter when or how you believe; it only matters who you believe in. Doubts, questions, thoughts, and accusations will always be part of your mental and spiritual makeup. To some degree, they are part of everybody's. The truth is, we are fragile, and we are fighting a very real war against a powerful enemy who loves to assault our minds.

At one time in my life, when the Devil accused me of not believing as I should, I would remind him that I did not believe in my believing; I believed in Jesus Christ. I had made Christ my substitute, and, as far as I was concerned, even Jesus' faith was a substitute for mine. As I grew in my faith, however, I quit reminding the Devil of anything. I just ignored him, no longer considering him worthy of my time.

Before I close this chapter, I would like to address the biblical terminologies for faith. The words, faith, believe, receive, believe on, believe in, call on, and trust, etc. are essentially just different ways of saying the same thing: faith. Faith is not like some describe. Faith is not "falling into the arms of Jesus" and trusting him to "catch you." And it is not some big "leap of faith" we're supposed to work up one day.

Faith (believing) is composed of two things. First, it is your conviction that a certain thing is true. In this case, it is your sincere conviction that Jesus Christ is the Son of God who died on the cross for your sins.

Second, faith is trust (reliance). So, you not only have to believe the gospel is true, but you must rely on the truth that you believe. Satan, for example, knew who God was, but he rejected God's love and care and put his trust in himself. Judas Iscariot also knew who Jesus was, but he rejected Jesus as his Savior. He put his trust in silver, instead of in Christ.

In the same way, there are many who sincerely believe Jesus died for them, yet who choose to rely on other things for eternal life instead of (or in addition to) the salvation Jesus has accomplished. I grew up in church, so I always believed in who Christ was, but I did not always rely on what Christ did. Instead, I relied on the prayer I prayed, my surrendered life, and on the sincerity of my heart.

Merely believing that Jesus is the Savior of the world is like remaining outside the ark Noah built. You see ark, and you know it's there, but you will drown if you don't take shelter in the ark that you know. A person is saved when that person not only believes the salvation Jesus accomplished through His death and resurrection, but when he accepts (relies on) that salvation for himself.

Have you determined in your heart to accept the death and shed blood of Jesus Christ as the full and complete atonement for your sin? If you have, then you have the same salvation Abraham, Moses, the twelve apostles, and I have. Christians are just people who are taking God at His Word—trusting that Jesus did what He said He did, and we are waiting on Him to come and do what He said He will do.

Finally, don't ever confuse faith with peace. I have trusted Christ as my Savior for many years now. At certain times over the years, I have sensed great peace and security while meditating on the cross. At other times, I've been assaulted greatly by the Devil and had doubts about various things. When I was assaulted by the Devil, it was not a peaceful experience, but that doesn't mean I wasn't trusting in Jesus during those times. Once I decided to trust Jesus as my savior, I have never made the conscientious decision to no longer have Him as my Savior. And I never will.

Suppose a dad drops his teenage daughter off near a park bench just outside a shopping center. He tells her, "Honey, I'll be here at this park bench to pick you up before the shopping center closes tonight." She agrees and then goes inside to shop. Several hours later, she makes her way back to the park bench where her dad said he would meet her. She waits for half an hour, but he's not there.

Eventually, many of the cars in the parking lot leave, and her dad still hasn't arrived. She gets nervous, but she reminds herself of the words her father told her before he left, and she stays on that park bench. It's now ten minutes till closing time, and some of her friends who are leaving the store offer to give her a ride home.

"Maybe he forgot," they say. "Maybe he had an accident. Let us take you home."

She thinks about it but declines. "No, my dad said he will be here to pick me up before closing, so I will stay here and wait on him."

When her friends leave, she gets a little scared. She starts to doubt, but she stays put. And, finally, just before the shopping center closes, her dad pulls up to the park bench to pick her up, and she leaves happily with him.

Even during her times of doubt, she never left the bench. She never quit believing the words of her father. And, if you have put your trust in Jesus, you may have gone through a lot of fear and doubt in your life, but you've never left the bench. Sure, you are frightened at times, when the Devil whispers things that make you afraid. But there you are, still on that park bench, waiting on Jesus to come back, just like He said.

27 WHAT IF GOD IS NO LONGER DEALING WITH MY HEART?

Just a few hours before I sat down to write this chapter, a forty-year-old man from North Carolina wrote to me, asking for help. He was afraid he may have missed his opportunity to be saved.

When he was thirteen years old, an invitation to "come forward" and "get saved" was given in a church service. But, being the shy little boy he was, he didn't go forward. Now that he is grown, he fears he cannot be saved, because (he said) God may never deal with his heart again, like He did during the "invitation" time.

Like this man, people sometimes fear their opportunity to be saved has passed them by, because they did not go down to the "altar" when they were "under conviction." Being "under conviction" is a phrase that's sometimes used to describe certain feelings experienced during an "altar call." Sweaty palms, trembling, fear, discomfort, and that deep churning in your stomach are just a few things you may experience during the so-called invitation time. After all, it's hard not to experience these things when emotionally stirring music is being played, and the preacher is telling you that you may go to hell if you don't come down to the "altar".

Eager to get people to the "altar," preachers will sometimes tell the congregation that, to be saved, God must draw them by His Holy Spirit. They warn the congregation, saying, "If God is dealing with your heart, you need to come to the altar now, because God may never 'knock on your heart's door' again." Of course, the Holy Spirit does draw us to Jesus. But, as we saw in a previous chapter, He draws us by convincing us of our sin, of the truth of the gospel, and of our need to believe on Jesus.

Remember, Jesus said the Holy Spirit *"will reprove the world of sin, and of righteousness, and of judgment"* (John 16:8). I routinely speak to people who are reproved (convicted) of sin, righteousness, and judgment. They know they are sinners; they believe the gospel; they know Jesus is the way, the truth, and the life, and they want desperately to be saved. But, because they are not experiencing the same feelings they once had during an "altar call," they fear God is no longer "convicting" or "drawing" them to Jesus. So they fear there is no hope left for them—they fear they have "sinned away the day of grace."

If you are one of these people, then you need to know there is a big difference between the intense feelings generated by emotional music and high-pressure preaching, and the actual conviction of the Holy Spirit. Countless people have gone down to the "altar" with these feelings who were never saved. But those the Holy Spirit draws will be convinced of their need for the gospel, and (with or without these feelings) they will go to the cross and live forever.

If you are convinced that you are a sinner; if you are convinced that Jesus died for your sins and rose again; if you are convinced that you can only be saved through what Jesus has done; and if you seek to believe on Him and be justified by His blood alone, then rest assured, the Holy Spirit of God is drawing you to Jesus. That's His work and His work alone. No preacher, or any other person, including yourself, can convince the heart of its need for Jesus Christ.

While in the middle of writing this chapter, I was contacted by a woman from Iowa who was afraid she had "crossed the line" and God had given her up. After years of wrestling with assurance of her salvation, struggling with sin, and battling a fear of going to hell, this woman was beginning to grow numb to the things of God.

This numbness is a phenomenon I have frequently encountered in people who have undergone a lengthy battle with doubt. Their conscience, which was once tender toward sin, gradually begins to grow dull. And the strong urges they once experienced to pursue God begin to fade away. In fact, sometimes they feel they just don't care anymore, and they are afraid their ambivalence toward God is a sign that God has given them over to a reprobate mind, such as the kind spoken of in Romans 1.

"Isn't there a point when God will quit dealing with a person and turn that person over to a reprobate mind?" this woman asked me.

I responded with a kind and comforting laugh. "Of course, but you have not been turned over to a reprobate mind."

"Why do you laugh?" she asked.

I told her, "Think about it. You have searched out and contacted a complete stranger who lives 1,000 miles away from you, because you want to know for sure that you are saved and on your way to heaven. If you are not a soul thirsting for salvation, I don't know who is. And Jesus said in John 7:37, *If any man thirst, let him come unto me, and drink.*'"

Reader, if you are afraid God may have given up on you, rest assured, He hasn't. A reprobate person isn't afraid of having a reprobate mind. If you want to be saved, it's because God wants you to be saved. Your desire for Christ is simply God's desire for you.

I believe the loss of feeling that so many people experienced is due to a survival mechanism God has given us. After a prolonged period of time, we tend to suppress our emotions, lest we be overcome by them and be unable to function. I have experienced prolonged sorrows to the point that I have cried until I couldn't cry anymore. I was numb, yet even with the dullness of my emotions, I still cared very much about the situation I was in. Is it not the same with you?

Suppose you had a big red button in front of you right now. All you had to do was push that button and you would be saved. Would you push it? Most assuredly you would, right? I mean, feeling or no feeling, you would jump at the chance to push that button, because that's your true desire. Revelation 22:17 says, "*. . . whosoever will, let him take the water of life freely.*"

Feeling or no feeling, if you *will* then you may *take* the living water of Jesus Christ! So take Jesus now, not because you have emotions, but because you have an invitation from God to do so.

28 THE DEVIL'S TREADMILL

Have you ever run on the Devil's "treadmill"? It all starts when the Devil puts one doubtful thought into your mind. He leans over to you and whispers, "What if the Bible is not true?"

This thought disturbs you, so you immediately feel the need to respond to it. Like rushing to put out a fire, you begin reminding yourself of the trustworthiness of God's Word. You remember the fulfilled prophecies in the Bible, and the eyewitness accounts of the apostles, who not only recorded what Jesus said and did but who willingly gave their lives for the message they preached. Surely, no one would knowingly die for a lie.

So, you tell yourself, "The Bible is the Word of God, and I believe it!" But the Devil still won't leave you alone.

Because lies are manufactured, the Devil has a continual supply of them. So, once you have overcome one lie, he simply whispers another lie into your ear. "Okay, you believe the Bible is God's Word, but how do you know you believe it correctly? What about this doctrine or that doctrine?"

So, you study the Bible. You search the commentaries, and you search the web, trying to make sure you understand whatever issue(s) the Devil is troubling you with. And, once you have assured yourself on those issues, the Devil will quit causing you to doubt the *Bible*, and he will start causing you to doubt *yourself* instead.

The Devil will blow a cold wind across your heart; he will put wicked thoughts into your mind, and he will sorely tempt you to sin. And, when you *do* sin, he will say to you, "Look at you! You are not living like a child of God! You are not saved!" Then you will wrestle with that fear for a long while.

Eventually, you will remind yourself that we are not saved by our works but by the work of Jesus Christ. And you will gain victory over that doubt. But as soon as you overcome that doubt, the Devil will speak many more troubling things into your ear: "You don't have the joy Christians should have," "You don't measure up," "You don't have a strong assurance of salvation," "You don't love God as you should," "You don't really believe."

Over and over, thoughts like these will come into your head. And, because you feel the need to answer every one of them, you will pour time, energy, emotions, prayers, and tears into answering these nagging doubts.

And after you have responded to the very last doubt, the battle is still not over. Because, like the belt on a treadmill, the Devil will start over at the beginning, and he will run you through the same old doubts all over again.

Responding to the Devil will never solve your doubts. In fact, as long as you keep responding to every doubt he puts into your mind, he will keep putting them into your mind. If you keep taking the bait, the Devil will keep casting the lure. And you will be like a runner on a treadmill who grows exhausted but gets nowhere.

If you are experiencing this problem, the solution is simple: get off the treadmill. Quit responding to every accusation the Devil makes. When we study the life of Jesus, we learn a valuable truth, namely, we owe no answer to the enemy.

Mark 15:3-5 says, *"the chief priests accused him of many things: but he answered nothing. And Pilate asked him again, saying, Answer you nothing? behold how many things they witness against you. But Jesus yet answered nothing . . ."*

Jesus knew that no matter what He told His enemies, there would never be an answer good enough for them. Why? Because His enemies didn't come to *learn* from Him; they came to *destroy* Him. Likewise, no answer you give the Devil will make him leave you alone. You will never satisfy him; you will never convince him; you will never talk him into submission because, as John 10:10 says, *"The thief comes not, but for to steal, and to kill, and to destroy . . ."*

While writing this chapter, I was speaking to a man about his salvation. He told me, "I know the Bible is true, and I know Jesus died for my sins. But, even though I know this to be true, my mind tells me Jesus died for everybody else's sins but mine."

Notice, then, how the man knew the truth, but his mind contradicted what he knew he believed. And, even though he tried answering his doubts with the Word of God, his mind would sometimes get so troubled with doubt, so filled with arguments against him, until the Devil's lies completely overwhelmed him.

To get off the Devil's treadmill, you have to know which voice to listen to. You must listen to the voice that *confirms* the Word of God, not the voice that *contradicts* it. It is an age-old strategy of the Devil to contradict the Word of God. And, since the Devil cannot overthrow the Word of God, he will try to over shout it.

In 1 Kings 22, the king of Israel asked the king of Judah to go with him into battle. The king of Judah was willing to help, but he wanted to check with God first to make sure God wanted him in the battle. We pick up the story in verse 6: *"the king of Israel gathered the prophets together, about four hundred men, and said unto them, Shall I go against Ramothgilead to battle, or shall I forbear? And they said, Go up; for the Lord shall deliver it into the hand of the king."*

Wow. Four hundred men. That's a lot of prophets! And all these prophets said the same thing: "Go fight, and you will win!" But there was something about these prophets that made the king of Judah uneasy, so he asked the king of Israel, *"Is there not here a prophet of the Lord besides, that we might enquire of him?"*

Jehoshaphat, the king of Judah, wanted to be sure he was doing God's will. He didn't want a pep rally full of false prophets; he wanted to hear from a real prophet so he could know the true will of God. So he asked the King of Israel if there was another prophet in Israel besides those four hundred men.

We pick back up with verse 8: *"the king of Israel said unto Jehoshaphat, There is yet one man, Micaiah the son of Imlah, by whom we may enquire of the Lord: but I hate him; for he does not prophesy good concerning me, but evil . . ."*

There were four hundred false prophets, but Micaiah was the only man who spoke the true Word of God. The king of Israel, however, was a wicked man. He did not like Micaiah, because Micaiah told the truth, whether the king liked it or not. Contrary to the four hundred prophets, when Micaiah was called, he told the kings to not go to battle, for it was not the will of God.

The King of Judah had to decide, therefore, which voice he would listen to—the voice that spoke the *loudest* or the voice that spoke the *truth*. If you are familiar with the story, then you know how it ends. The lying prophets withstood Micaiah and struck him on the face. And the kings chose to listen to the lying majority. They put Micaiah in prison and the kings lost the battle.

On another occasion, in Numbers 14, Israel sent twelve spies to spy out the land of Canaan. God had told them to go in and conquer the land. God said He would win the battle for them. It was God's free gift, and all Israel had to do was take it. But when the twelve spies came back, ten of those spies told the people they could not win the battle, because the Canaanites were too big for them to defeat. Out of those twelve spies, only two told the truth. Only two confirmed the Word of God and encouraged the people to take the land.

Once again, the people had a decision to make. Would they listen to the ten spies that *contradicted* God's Word? Or would they listen to the two spies that *confirmed* it? Like the king of Judah, the people of Israel made the mistake of listening to the loudest voice. Instead of believing God's Word, which promised them victory, they doubted God's Word, and *"all the congregation lifted up their voice, and cried; and the people wept that night"* (Numbers 14:1).

Maybe you have ten spies of your own, and they have caused you to weep much, too. Like the king of Judah, and like the people of Israel, you must decide which voice you will listen to. You must choose to either listen to the doubts, thoughts, and feelings that contradict God's Word or to the Scriptures that confirm it.

And, remember, you don't owe the enemy an answer. Those two spies could not convince the ten, and Micaiah could not convince the four hundred. Even so, you will never convince the ten spies in your head, and you will never persuade the four hundred false prophets that torment your mind. So quit responding to them. Instead, like Jesus, answer them nothing, and listen only to the still small voice of God's Word. Victory does not come by defeating the lies but by accepting the truth.

29 CONQUERING THE CONFLICT WITHIN YOU

If you have come to a full understanding of the gospel and have placed your faith in Jesus, yet you still doubt your salvation, then your problem could be more with your mind than with your spirit. The mind is a powerful thing, and it is often the culprit that causes doubt. This is especially true if you have struggled with doubts for an extended period of time.

Consider the combat soldier. After returning home from battle, combat soldiers will occasionally suffer from post-traumatic stress disorder (PTSD). They may suffer from flashbacks, emotional numbing, sleep disorders, panic attacks, depression, and many other symptoms, all because of the horrific events they experienced during battle. But, the important thing to remember is, these are *post*-traumatic symptoms, which means they are suffering from these things, *after* the battle is over, while in the safety of their own home.

Compare the experience of the combat soldier to those who've suffered from severe and prolonged doubt of their salvation. While the combat soldier faces a mortal enemy, those who doubt their salvation battle a much greater foe. Ephesians 6:12 explains it this way, *"For we wrestle not against flesh and blood, but against principalities, against powers, against the rulers of the darkness of this world, against spiritual wickedness in high places."*

The combat soldier may experience the loss of limb, the loss of life, and the fear of physical death. But people who doubt their salvation fear something greater—they fear losing both body and soul in hell. Some of them go for decades, living in constant fear that, at any moment, they will draw their last breath and burn forever in the lake of fire. For these people, the battle is very real, and the greatest casualties are at stake.

Anyone who experiences an extremely traumatic event may develop PTSD. And women are twice as likely as men to do so. Therefore, like a combat soldier, people who doubt their salvation may struggle with PTSD, even after they are saved and the battle is over.

After coming home from battle, a soldier may wake up in a panic and have to remind himself that he is safe in bed and no longer in danger. In the same way, those who've struggled with doubt may wake up in a panic and have to remind themselves that they are safe in Jesus and no longer in danger of going to hell. Experiencing fear and panic isn't an indication that you're not saved, any more than it means the soldier is not safe at home.

If you have accepted Christ as your Savior, you are "safe at home," but the battle in your mind may continue for some time. As certain things may trigger symptoms in a combat soldier, so certain things may trigger symptoms in you. I have spoken to many people who, though they know they trust in Christ, still continue to occasionally experience fear and anxiety during "altar calls" or whenever they hear sermons that question people's salvation.

Emotional numbing is another symptom I frequently encounter in the people I counsel. In order to survive traumatic stress, people must be able to compartmentalize their thoughts. If fear and anxiety were to continue at the forefront of their minds, they would lose their ability to function and survive. This is why people at funerals are able to laugh when someone tells a funny story about a loved one who just passed away. Their minds are compartmentalizing the pain, and this allows them to both laugh and cry at the appropriate times.

But if the trauma is severe enough, and lasts long enough, our minds can grow numb to the pain. It's as if the brain is sedating our emotional senses so we can continue to function. People will sometimes mistake this emotional numbing as an indication that they no longer care for God. But this is not true. Even though they can no longer feel the fear, they are, in fact, more afraid than ever before.

I have heard from people who were terrified that they no longer desired to go to heaven or were no longer afraid of going to hell. They were terrified that they were no longer terrified. But, the truth was, they did care; it's just that their senses had grown numb to the pain.

I have spoken to many other people who suffered from a different sort of internal conflict. Generally speaking, they have no doubt about the Bible, about God, or about the gospel. Their struggle is with themselves. They carry a measuring tape on their person and are always pulling it out to measure themselves.

And when they do, they find that they come short of what they should be. They find fault with their faith, with their repentance, with their works, their love, their understanding, their sincerity, and nearly everything else. They even find fault with their awareness and perception as a person.

Since the Bible says the heart of man is *"deceitful above all things,"* they begin to wonder if they truly want Jesus. They lose the ability to trust their own desires, even the thoughts of their own hearts. They wonder if the choices they make are really their choices. Thus, they may choose to accept Christ as their Savior, yet begin to wonder if that was their choice, or if they were deceived into thinking it was their choice.

I have been asked, "How can I know I have really chosen Christ as my Savior?" and "How can I know I really want to be saved?" If you struggle with this, let me ask you a question I sometimes ask them—it's the one I asked in Chapter 27.

Suppose you had a big red button in front of you right now. All you had to do was push that button and you would be immediately saved forever. Would you push it?

Every time I have asked this question, I've gotten the same answer. People always say they would push the button. I bet you would, too. In fact, you would probably push it right away, wouldn't you? And, if you would push this button, then Jesus is clearly your choice. So, stand firm on that choice.

We are imperfect people. So if you measure yourself, you will never measure up. Your faith, your repentance, your love, your devotion, your prayers, or whatever you measure about yourself—it will never satisfy you, for it will always *"come short of the glory of God"* (Romans 3:23). This is why God gave His perfect Son, so we could "measure up" in Him, just as 2 Corinthians 5:21 says, *"For He has made Him who knew no sin, to be sin for us, that we might become the righteousness of God in him."*

When we accept Jesus, God accepts us. The gospel is not about you measuring up; it is about God measuring Jesus instead of you.

So, if you are struggling with this issue, you need to stop looking at yourself and start looking at Jesus. When people doubt their salvation, it is almost always because they are measuring themselves, when they should be measuring the work of Jesus on the cross. Speaking of the cross, Isaiah 53:11 says, *"He shall see of the travail of his soul, and shall be satisfied . . ."*

Why is God satisfied when He sees Jesus? Because, when God saw Jesus suffering on the cross, He saw justice being served; He saw the law being fulfilled, and He saw everything in Jesus that He could ever want to see in you. So quit measuring yourself, my friend. If God is satisfied with Jesus, you should be satisfied with Jesus, too.

Obsessive Compulsive Disorder (OCD) is another enemy of the mind that may cause people to doubt their salvation. OCD is an anxiety disorder in which people have unwanted and repeated thoughts, feelings, and obsessions. I have spoken to otherwise intelligent people who were so plagued with obsessions like this that their minds would never let them rest in Christ as they should.

I spoke to one such woman, who continually thought she was committing the unpardonable sin. Even the most basic functions in life would throw her into a panic. On one occasion, she was about to purchase an item in a clothing store. Just as she was about to swipe her credit card, she wondered if the article of clothing had been manufactured in a sweatshop. She wanted the clothes, but she didn't want to support a sweatshop. She hesitated, but then purchased the clothing anyway.

Afterward, she was afraid her purchase may have been a rejection of Jesus, and she feared she was doomed to hell. To someone in her right mind, this type of fear makes no sense at all. But to people with OCD, thoughts like this can continually plague them.

I am a firm believer in the power of the Holy Spirit to set us free from these things. But I also know there are some very broken people out there, who are not only broken spiritually but physically, too. And these people may benefit from the medication of a good psychiatrist, in addition to the message of a good evangelist.

Whatever your inner conflict is, just remember that God loves both the weak and the strong. 1 Thessalonians 5:14 tells us to, *"comfort the feebleminded, support the weak . . ."*

So if you are one of the weak, don't be afraid. Jesus knows your frailties, and He is strong on your behalf. If a psychiatrist cannot help you, or if you cannot afford one, be of good cheer: the grace of God reaches where medicine cannot.

30 FRUIT INSPECTING

You shall know them by their fruits. (Matthew 7:16)

Perhaps you've heard that we are supposed to be fruit inspectors. The term "fruit inspecting" comes from Jesus' words in Matthew 7:15-16, where Jesus, speaking of false prophets, said, *"Beware of false prophets, which come to you in sheep's clothing, but inwardly they are ravening wolves. You shall know them by their fruits."*

So, in this verse, fruit inspecting is not about looking at ourselves for evidence of salvation but about determining if a person is a false prophet. Just a few chapters later, Jesus gave us an example of what real fruit inspecting is when false prophets rejected Him and blasphemed the Holy Spirit.

Here's what Jesus told them in Matthew 12:32-33: *"And whosoever speaks a word against the Son of man, it shall be forgiven him: but whosoever speaks against the Holy Ghost, it shall not be forgiven him, neither in this world, neither in the world to come. Either make the tree good, and his fruit good; or else make the tree corrupt, and his fruit corrupt: for the tree is known by his fruit."*

By rejecting God's Word, they were clearly not God's prophets. Though they pretended to be a good tree, their bad fruit betrayed their hypocrisy. So fruit inspecting is not about gaining assurance of our salvation by inspecting our good works; it's about looking for discrepancies between what a "man of God" claims to be, and what that man actually does with what God says.

Trying to gain assurance of your salvation by looking at how good you are is not "fruit inspecting"; it's just another way of measuring yourself instead of Jesus. It is a trap, and if you let yourself fall into it, you may find it difficult to get out of.

Sometimes young Christians want to "bear fruit" so they can see "evidence" of their salvation. This evidence, they think, will give them the assurance that they're saved. So these young (or immature) believers will start performing Christian tasks to try to gain assurance. But behaving like a Christian doesn't make us Christians; faith in Christ makes us Christians. Thus, our assurance doesn't come by knowing what we have done but by knowing what Christ has done.

Of course, we should all bear fruit. But bearing fruit doesn't come by trying; it comes by abiding. It comes by resting our faith in Jesus; by accepting His Word and His cross as the only evidence of salvation we need. The Bible says we walk by faith. Therefore, our Christian walk (bearing fruit) comes by resting our faith in the death and resurrection of Christ.

Getting this backwards, Christians can fall into the trap of knowing they must believe in Christ to be saved but feeling like they have to work ("bear fruit") in order to prove they are saved. Don't make this mistake. If you work to know you are saved, then you will soon wonder if your faith is in Jesus or in your work. Thus, what you thought would give you assurance, will actually give you more doubt.

In John 15:5, Jesus said, "*I am the vine, you are the branches: He that abides in me, and I in him, the same brings forth much fruit: for without me you can do nothing.*" Did you catch that? *"you can do nothing."*

Do you know what that means? It means you couldn't bear fruit if you tried. Fruit is not our work; it is Jesus' work. Our part is to abide (in Christ); Jesus' part is to produce fruit.

Look to the cross. See the love God has for you there. See Jesus as He gives His life for you.

Watch Him bleeding for you, dying for you, and suffering God's judgment for your sin. Watch Him, as He fully satisfies God on your behalf. Look at Him, as He takes your sin and gives God His righteousness on your behalf. Watch Him as He conquers death for you and enters heaven to guarantee your future arrival. Watch Him, and you will know that you can *"do nothing,"* but Jesus has done it all.

If you will make Jesus the assurance of your salvation (abide in Him and what He has done for you), then you will have *"faith that works by love"* (Galatians 5:6). Then, and only then, will you finally be free to serve Christ as you desire. Until we are satisfied with Jesus' work *for* us, we cannot experience Jesus work *in* us.

31 CAN I LOSE MY SALVATION?

Perhaps the most powerful verse on eternal security is John 5:24, in which Jesus said, *"Verily, verily, I say unto you, He that hears my word, and believes on him that sent me, has everlasting life, and shall not come into condemnation; but is passed from death unto life."*

Jesus said he who hears His word and trusts God for the salvation He accomplished, has (at this present time) everlasting life and shall not come into condemnation, but has been passed from death unto life. Notice that He said the person who *"has everlasting life"* (is saved in the present) *"shall not come into condemnation"* (shall not be lost in the future). This is very clear. This makes perfect sense. For if a person with "everlasting" life could lose his or her salvation, then the life that person had obviously wasn't "everlasting."

The eternal security of the believer is based on God's unfailing purpose of the gospel. Namely, all who believe in Christ for salvation are predestined to be made like Him.

Romans 8:29-30 makes it clear that salvation is both eternal and irrevocable. Pay close attention to the following verses: *"For whom he did foreknow, he also did predestinate to be conformed to the image of his Son, that he might be the firstborn among many brethren. Moreover whom he did predestinate, them he also called: and whom he called, them he also justified: and whom he justified, them he also glorified."*

Salvation is given to us according to the foreknowledge of God. Without getting into all the details, let me just say that God knows beforehand who will believe in Christ and who will not. And those whom God knows will believe in Christ, He predestinates them (determines them ahead of time) to be conformed to the image of Jesus (to be made perfect like Him).

The words *"he also"* in these verses are vital, because they show the unbreakable links between the foreknowledge of God (our election) and our ultimate destiny of being made like Jesus (our glorification).

In Romans 5, Paul said God justifies us by our faith in Jesus. And, then, in Romans 8, Paul explained that those whom God justifies *"he also"* glorifies. This means God will not only justify (declare innocent) all who believe in Christ as their Savior, but *"he also"* will glorify them (make them perfect like Jesus).

And, Paul went on to say, if God has justified us by faith, then *"he also"* has called us. And He called us because *"he also"* predestinated us to be made like Jesus, because He foreknew us before the world began.

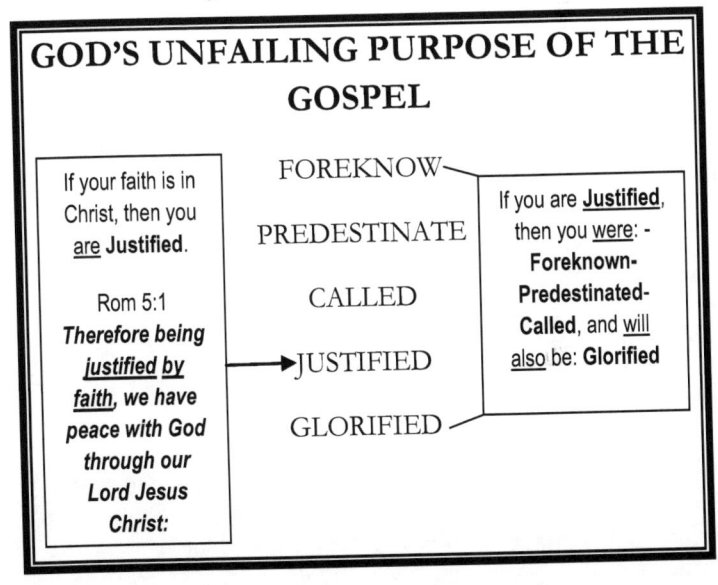

GOD'S UNFAILING PURPOSE OF THE GOSPEL

If your faith is in Christ, then you **are Justified**. Rom 5:1 **Therefore being justified by faith, we have peace with God through our Lord Jesus Christ:**	FOREKNOW PREDESTINATE CALLED →JUSTIFIED GLORIFIED	If you are **Justified**, then you were: - **Foreknown-Predestinated-Called**, and will also be: **Glorified**

I have studied our beloved gospel for a long time, and I have never seen a verse in the Bible that says you can lose your salvation. Nor have I found an example in the Bible of someone losing his or her salvation. If you think Judas lost his salvation, you are wrong. Judas was never saved. John 6:70-71 says, *"Jesus answered them, Have not I chosen you twelve, and one of you is a devil? He spake of Judas Iscariot the son of Simon: for he it was that should betray him, being one of the twelve."*

Judas was an apostle of Jesus, but he was not saved. He was a *"devil"*—an adversary of Jesus. Judas is not an example of how someone can lose his or her salvation; he is an example of how a lost hypocrite can occupy the highest office in the church, fool the crowd, and then die and go to hell.

Bible verses that may appear to say you can lose your salvation are actually talking about hypocrites like Judas. 2 Peter 2:20-22 is a good example:

> *For if after they have escaped the pollutions of the world through the knowledge of the Lord and Savior Jesus Christ, they are again entangled therein, and overcome, the latter end is worse with them than the beginning. For it had been better for them not to have known the way of righteousness, than, after they have known it, to turn from the holy commandment delivered unto them. But it is happened unto them according to the true proverb, The dog is turned to his own vomit again; and the sow that was washed to her wallowing in the mire.*

At first, Peter seems to be talking about people losing their salvation, but when you read it carefully you will see he is actually talking about people like Judas—people who became religious but who were never saved. In verse 22, Peter is talking about people who were *reformed* but who were not *regenerated*. In other words, they changed their behavior on the outside (like Judas), but their thinking had not been changed on the inside (like Christians). They changed their behavior, but they never changed their minds and trusted in Jesus.

To explain this, Peter used the illustration of a *"dog"* and a *"sow"* (hog). The dog got cleaned out, and the hog got cleaned up. The dog got rid of what made him feel bad on the inside, and the hog got rid of what made him look bad on the outside. But, at the end of the day, they were just dogs and hogs; they were not Jesus' sheep. They gave up drugs; they got a haircut; they joined the choir, but their old nature was still the same. So they fooled people for a while, but after a while (like the dog and the hog), they left Jesus and went back to what they really loved.

There are other scriptures people use to try to prove salvation can be lost, and we don't have time to cover every one of them. But if you will remember that the Bible promises eternal life to all who believe, and if you will carefully study the scriptures that appear to say you can lose your salvation, I believe you will see that they are referring to the same people Peter was referring to in the above passage.

I used to be afraid of Hebrews Chapters 6 and 10, which talk about damnation for those who *"fall away"* or *"sin willfully"* after receiving the knowledge of the truth. I knew I had willfully sinned before (who hasn't?), so those chapters really concerned me. But when I studied the book of Hebrews, I learned that the writer was talking about a specific sin. He was talking about the sin of, after being enlightened to the truth of Jesus' sacrifice on the cross, willfully rejecting His sacrifice and turning back to the Old Testament animal sacrifices.

> *For it is impossible for those who were once enlightened, and have tasted of the heavenly gift, and were made partakers of the Holy Ghost, And have tasted the good word of God, and the powers of the world to come, If they shall fall away, to renew them again unto repentance; seeing they crucify to themselves the Son of God afresh, and put him to an open shame. For the earth which drinks in the rain that comes often upon it, and brings forth herbs suitable for them by whom it is dressed, receives blessing from God: But that which bears thorns and briers is rejected, and is nigh unto cursing; whose end is to be burned.* (Hebrews 6:4-8)

Some people believe the *"falling away"* in this passage speaks of backsliding people who lose their salvation. They teach that these people can never be saved again because Jesus would have to die on the cross again for their sins and be "crucified afresh."

But this is not what these verses are saying. The passage is talking about people who were *"enlightened"* and who *"tasted."* In other words, as light gives knowledge to the eyes, and as taste gives knowledge to the tongue, so these people had received the knowledge of Christ in their minds.

However, after receiving that wonderful knowledge, they willfully rejected the truth of the gospel (as someone might close their eyes to the light or spit out what they tasted). To explain this, the writer uses the example of how rain falls upon the earth. Even though different parcels of ground receive the same rain, some ground bears fruit, while other ground bears thorns and briers.

The point is, just as the same rain can fall upon different parcels of land, and each parcel can bear either fruit or briers, so the same gospel can fall upon the ears of different people (enlighten them), and those people will either accept the gospel (bear fruit) or willfully reject the gospel (bear thorns and briers).

Willfully rejecting the gospel is the sin Hebrews 10:26 is speaking about, which says, *"For if we sin willfully after that we have received the knowledge of the truth, there remains no more sacrifice for sins . . ."*

Since animal sacrifices cannot take away our sin, Jesus' sacrifice is the only sacrifice that can. So if we willfully reject the sacrifice of Jesus, *"after that we have received the knowledge of the truth, there remains no more sacrifice for sins . . ."* This is not talking about someone *losing* his or her salvation; this is talking about someone willfully *rejecting* it. Therefore, if you willfully accept the sacrifice of Christ, then you are a believer; you have eternal life, and these scriptures do not apply to you.

Some people might argue, "But if we tell people they can't lose their salvation, then they won't be afraid of going to hell, and they will go out and sin all they want to." Actually, the truth is just the opposite. Everybody sins, but Christians understand that sin is harmful to them. Though they are tempted to sin, they don't want to continue in it; they want to overcome it. And, 1 John 5:4 says, *"this is the victory that overcomes the world, even our faith."*

So it is *faith* (not *fear*) that overcomes our sin. Serving God because we are afraid of going to hell is not faith working by love; it is fear working by the law. And *"the law is not of faith"* (Galatians 3:12).

When we are confident that we are eternally secure by the sacrifice of Jesus, we will become humbled by His mercy and grateful for what He's done for us. We will love Him because He first loved us, and we will serve Him boldly with a grateful heart. But when we lack this confidence, we will lack the strength that comes through a full and mature faith in His finished work for us on the cross, and we will struggle with sin more because of it. So the doctrine of eternal security doesn't *encourage* sin; it actually *overcomes* it.

32 LETTERS FROM OTHERS

Since we learn from the experiences of others, I thought you might gain some insight by reading some of the correspondence I've had with people who've written me for help. Below, you will find excerpts from a few emails I've received, along with my response to their particular concerns. Reading these will allow you to identify with their problems, see that you are not alone, and hopefully benefit from the advice they were given.

A letter from "Greg":

> First of all, I would like to talk about my conversion experience. I was 14 years old, and I had been denying Christ for more than two years because of my prideful nature. During an altar call while my father was preaching, I can't remember if I felt a pull to the altar or not; but I heard a voice inside my head that said, "I can save you." So ... I was about to walk to the front to pray and accept Christ, but I swiftly turned around and went to the bathroom. I went to the bathroom and looked in the mirror, yet that voice said the same thing again ("I can save you"). I then got on my knees and prayed for Jesus to save me. After I prayed that prayer, the voice said, "That's it, you're saved." Furthermore, as soon as I stepped up from praying, I started to doubt that experience, and it seemed like Satan himself was standing there fueling it. I began to believe that I did not get saved that day, but a part of me

inside believed that I did, and it was hard for me not to believe that I did not get saved. I never did go up that day to tell people I got saved in the bathroom. During that week, I struggled with doubt of my salvation. Then the next Sunday came, and I was overwhelmed by doubt. I was doubled-minded like James talks about in the first chapter of his book. I then went to the altar to pray during an altar call, and everyone surrounded me. All I could hear was their sniffling and joyful weeping. I prayed and asked Jesus to save me, yet the voice I heard in my head wasn't saying, "I can save you." It said, "I already have." Therefore, I stood up and said I was saved.

Fast forward a couple of years and I'm a senior in high school. I had just recommitted my life, because doubt had eventually made me feel like I was cut off from God. I was very active in my local church, announced my calling to preach, and was growing spiritually. I was praying one day before Wednesday night services, and I prayed, "Lord, whatever you want me to do to lead more people to you, then I will do it. Even if that means you pull me up to the altar." We were having a youth lesson, and at the end of it the teacher for that night gave an altar call. Then there it was, the pull, a pull to the altar. Yet, while being "pulled" to the altar, I did not have in my mind that I needed to go get saved. I just knew God wanted me to go up there, but I didn't. As soon as I didn't go, the teacher said, "Maybe you've always thought you were saved but you're not." I eventually began to freak out and was full of fear. I did not go to the altar, and a voice shot through my head that said, "You denied Me." This voice gave me fear as well.

Ever since that night, doubt has absolutely killed me, and it feels like I'm close to God, but it also feels like doubt is trying to kill me spiritually. I've talked to multiple people (very close friends and pastors) about this situation, and they told me it was God answering my prayer. Also, they said God would never persecute someone like that or confuse a person about their salvation. Also, I know the Holy Spirit has the convincing power to prove to someone that they're not saved. Therefore, if I was lost, would the Holy Spirit have convinced me immediately during the pull to the altar? I am so confused that it literally feels like I'm dying. Another point, God has moved mountains for me in prayer and proved once that I am saved by answering a huge prayer for me that happened the very next day. Yet, it's so hard for me to believe it. I don't know if this is a spiritual attack from Satan, or if I'm actually lost . . .

The above letter is a good example of how confusing modern "Christianity" can become when the gospel is not present. When Greg talked about his supposed salvation experience, and about the assurance of his salvation, I want you to notice that he spoke about "tugs," "pulls," "voices," "altars," and "answered prayers." But he never spoke about the gospel. Not once did he mention Jesus' payment for his sins. Since Greg was not focused on the unchanging accomplishment of Jesus' salvation on the cross, he was continually dealing with the ever-changing mysteries of voices, and pulls, and religious experiences.

My response:

Greg, you are clutching your experiences like a Catholic clutches rosary beads, hoping to find peace in them. But since there is no peace in the things we experience, you have no peace of your salvation. You thought an answered prayer may be proof that you are saved. But have you not prayed for God to take away your doubts?

Answered prayer is not assurance of salvation. If it was, then we could have seventy percent of our prayers answered and still only be seventy percent sure we were saved. I am in no way making light of any blessings God may have given you in life, but we cannot use our experiences as the basis of our assurance.

So, instead of looking back to what you've experienced in your life, you should be looking back to what Christ experienced on the cross. His work on the cross made peace between God and man. His blood assures us that our debt is paid, so we must accept that as the assurance of our salvation.

You asked me, "If I wasn't saved, would the Holy Spirit have 'pulled me' to the altar?" That is exactly why we don't have "altar calls" at my church. You are basing your salvation on "voices" and a "pull" to a New Testament "altar" that, in the New Testament

Bible, doesn't even exist.

You must stop building your hopes and fears on the imaginations of men. You have put your eyes on a New Testament "altar" that's not in the Bible and on experiences you can never validate. But God wants you to put your eyes on His Son.

Anything other than Jesus and His cross is a distraction to block your view of the salvation He's accomplished. It doesn't matter if you "freaked out," "changed," heard a "voice," or even if you levitated off your feet. There is only one thing that should matter to you: Jesus Christ and Him crucified.

The Bible says he that believes on Jesus is not condemned. If you believe on Him, then you are not condemned. It's that simple. If, however, you look to your experiences, then your faith will be in those experiences and not in Jesus.

The gospel tells you that Jesus Christ has paid for your sins. Suppose you eat at a restaurant, and you suddenly realize you have no money. A friend, whose dining at a nearby table, pays your bill for you and hands you the receipt. If you have the receipt in your hand, then you won't fear the cash register on your way out. But, on the other hand, if you are holding a napkin, a straw, or a fork in your hand as you leave, you will surely fear the register, because those things can't pay the bill.

Greg, you are afraid because you are clutching the napkins and straws on the table. And I am trying to get you to let go of those things and grab the receipt (of the cross). For, if you have the cross, you can boldly wave the receipt of Jesus' blood before the register of heaven!

A letter from "Amy":

Hello Richard,

> I just wanted to say thank you for all the information on your website. When listening to your testimony, it sounds much like myself, although I have only (I laugh when I say "only") been in turmoil for 10 months, not the long periods as you have. I get it when you say it is nothing "we" do to have salvation; it is all based on what Jesus did so long ago by his righteous death. I listened to your testimony, and you mentioned that you thought that if

only you could get the blood applied to your name, then you would be saved. I ask you, what exactly did you do for that to happen? Just *believe* that it is applied since you're a sinner and Jesus is a saving God? No prayers needed? Sorry if I sound ignorant to everything you said, since you said it's not a prayer that saves you. As humans, how do you accept the gift of Jesus' death without any "I" involvement, such as asking him to save us or asking for that gift to be applied to me? Is just the believing ("whosoever believeth in him should not perish, but have eternal life") the receiving?

My response:

Amy, as the Bible says, it is all a matter of faith. Biblical faith is depending on Jesus Christ. So, when we believe on Jesus, we are relying on Jesus, instead of relying on ourselves. Faith, then, only includes the "I involvement" (as you say) in the sense that I am relying on Jesus.

I depend on Christ, which means I am substituting His work for mine. In other words, I recognize that my work—my righteousness, my justification, and the atonement for sin I need, cannot be accomplished by me; so I depend on (believe on) Christ, who accomplished these things in my stead. I am not working up some leap of faith that I may trust God to do something to save me; I am resting (relying) on the work He's already done.

The "I involvement" you mentioned concerns our responsibility in salvation. I know what you mean. You're thinking, "Jesus did the work, but don't I have to do something?" Think of it this way: Our responsibility in salvation is our *response* to His *ability*.

God has given us a substitute (Jesus). Since Jesus is our substitute, God's *holiness* can accept us based on Jesus' sinless life, and God's *justice* can excuse us based on Jesus' condemnation. When we understand that we are sinners, then we can recognize that the only way God can see us as sinless in His eyes is if He judges us on the basis of Jesus and His cross. Understanding this, we can relinquish any dependence we have in our own merit, and we can depend on the merit of Jesus Christ instead.

When you choose to rely on Jesus, God knows your heart, and thus He sees that you have accepted the salvation of His Son. At that moment, it's like God acknowledges your choice and says to Himself, "Amy has accepted the salvation of my Son. I will now accept her based on Jesus, who died in her place and in whom I am well pleased."

Remember, Amy, the Bible says Jesus is our great high priest. A prophet is someone who represents God *to the people*, but a priest is someone who represents *the people to God*. With that in mind, read the following passage (below):

> *For Christ is not entered into the holy places made with hands, which are the figures of the true; but into heaven itself, now to appear in the presence of God for us: Nor yet that he should offer himself often, as the high priest enters into the holy place every year with blood of others; For then must he often have suffered since the foundation of the world: but now once in the end of the world has he appeared to put away sin by the sacrifice of himself. And as it is appointed unto men once to die, but after this the judgment: So Christ was once offered to bear the sins of many; and unto them that look for him shall he appear the second time without sin unto salvation.* (Hebrews 9:24-28)

Wow! That is so good! Notice that it said Jesus rose to *"appear in the presence of God for us"*. Our great high priest has left the world, the cross, and the grave, and He has gone into heaven to appear in our place (to represent us) before God. Oh, what a grand representation we have!

Amy, Jesus is there right now to argue His righteousness, His death, and His blood as an atonement for you. The gospel is a message from heaven, in which God offers you the opportunity to be represented by Jesus Christ. And "faith" is simply you accepting that gracious offer.

Amy, what is your response? Will you accept God's offer? Will you let Jesus represent you? Will you agree with God that you cannot be accepted by Him based on your own conduct? And will you now let God judge you on the basis of Jesus' conduct instead?

If you will rely on Jesus, then you will not be ashamed of that decision come judgment day, for the scripture says *"whoever believes on him shall not be ashamed"* (Romans 10:11). Will you now relinquish your faith in everything else, and accept Jesus Christ as your only hope for eternal life? Will you let God judge you on the basis of

Jesus' work instead of your own? If you will, then you are saved, for this is what it means to believe in Jesus; this is the essence of repentance and faith.

Amy, I know I am going to heaven because I have staked all my hope on one thing: Jesus. I am so glad God led me to make that decision. Will you make that decision, too? What is your answer?

A letter from a pastor and his wife:

> Hello, Bro Fulton. It's hard to say how we are doing. There are ups and downs. There are times when I feel at peace and that I am trusting Christ and then others when I feel afraid. I think what a part of me wants is an "experience." A moment when we know the lights have come on and the chains fall off for good; I guess a moment where we can know it "worked."
>
> But then I suppose that may not be the kind of faith the Lord is looking for. It's like when I can just focus on Christ and see myself resting in his arms, as it were, this brings comfort, and I have to think would also meet the demands of John 3:16, 36.
>
> I'd just like to be able to "stay there," and I find that to be challenging. I am troubled by questions like, "Why haven't you had an experience?" or "What if someone preached a hard message on hell? Wouldn't that still bother you?" or "Why don't you have perfect peace now?" Curious to hear your thoughts.

Notice how the pastor and his wife quoted more scripture and spoke more about the person of Christ than Greg. Due to their position in the church, they certainly had a better understanding of salvation than Greg. Nevertheless, they were weighted down with some religious baggage, which hindered them from resting in the salvation Jesus accomplished for them.

My response:

> "Pastor John," Rom 10:17 says, ". . . *faith comes by hearing, and hearing by the word of God.*" Faith (biblical/saving faith) comes by hearing the Word of God. When we hear the Word of God—the

good news of our salvation, we believe in Christ as our sin-bearer. And, since our faith is in Christ, we are saved. Watch how the scriptures bear witness to this:

Ephesians 1:13 says, *"In whom you also trusted, after that you heard the word of truth, the gospel of your salvation: in whom also after that you believed, you were sealed with that holy Spirit of promise..."*

So, being saved means we hear the good news (gospel) that Jesus died for our sins, and we accept the truth of that good news.

Acts 13:38-39 says, *"Be it known unto you therefore, men and brethren, that through this man is preached unto you the forgiveness of sins: And by him all that believe are justified from all things, from which you could not be justified by the law of Moses."*

If certain modern evangelists would have lived back in the apostles' day and would have witnessed people rejoicing after they heard the good news that Christ died for them, those evangelists would have stopped the people's celebration and told them they needed to ask Jesus to come into their hearts to save them. How confusing that would have been for them! One moment they are rejoicing because Jesus' death has saved them from the penalty of their sin, and the next moment they are told they must ask Jesus to save them (from the penalty of their sin).

The reason you're having trouble resting in the payment Jesus made for your sin is because you're trying to merge two conflicting ideas about the gospel. And these two ideas can never be reconciled, because one is biblical and the other is not.

A strong message on hell would not scare me, because it would be like me hearing a strong message on a home foreclosure. My house is paid for, so a message on home foreclosures won't rattle me one bit. In the same way, my sins are paid for, so a message on hell won't rattle me one bit.

I am now going to break your email down and respond to it in sections. Your words will be in italics, and mine in normal font.

It's hard to say how we are doing. There are ups and downs.

No, Brother. The cross has no ups and downs, just like the title on my home has no ups and downs. I'm not paid up one day and behind on my mortgage the next. The fact that my home is paid for is a matter of legal record. My mortgage has been paid in full. This is a constant and unchanging fact, regardless if I am thinking about that fact or if I have a peaceful feeling or experience about it or not.

So you must correct your thinking on this and align it with Scripture. Using your forever changing mental state as a barometer for a finished and unchanging gospel is like trying to measure the ocean by the current water level in your bathtub. One has no bearing on the other.

There are times when I feel at peace and that I am trusting Christ and then others when I feel afraid. I think what a part of me wants is an "experience." A moment when we know the lights have come on and the chains fall off for good; I guess a moment where we can know it "worked."

The moment we know it "worked" is the moment when Jesus cried, "It is finished" and then died. That is the moment everything worked, so that is the moment we look to and believe in. Remember, we are saved by Jesus' experience, not ours.

But then I suppose that may not be the kind of faith the Lord is looking for. It's like when I can just focus on Christ . . . this brings comfort, and I have to think would also meet the demands of John 3:16, 36.

Correct. Notice that when you consider Christ (as the Bible says), you have peace, but when you turn your eyes back on you, then you are troubled.

I'd just like to be able to "stay there," and I find that to be challenging.

It is not only challenging, but it's impossible with your current mindset. Can you imagine me struggling with my paid off mortgage? Could you imagine me wringing my hands in fear of having my home foreclosed and hoping I can keep hanging on and resting in my title deed? No! That's not resting at all.

That's you trying to get your faith to create drama and feelings for you. It's you (in your flesh) looking to the cross and saying, "Except I see signs and wonders I will not believe!" (John 4:48). I know that you are not trying to do this, but, in a sense, you are. Jesus said, *"It is finished"* (John 19:30). So rest, my brother, for the penalty has been paid, and the work's already done.

I am troubled by questions like, "Why haven't you had an experience?" or "What if someone preached a hard message on hell? Wouldn't that still bother you?" or "Why don't you have perfect peace now?"

You ask, "Why don't I have a perfect peace?" You DO have a perfect peace. Colossians 1:20 says Jesus *"made peace through the blood of his cross."* And Ephesians 2:14, says Jesus *"is our peace."*

So, peace is not a feeling; peace is a fact. Peace is a legal victory Jesus accomplished. Peace is about who Jesus is and what Jesus has done. And, though peace is not a feeling, I do feel good knowing what Jesus has done for me!

Sometimes, after nations sign peace treaties, the soldiers may keep fighting until news that the war is over has reached them. Like these soldiers, you are fighting a battle that's already been won. The war is over, Brother. Jesus has made peace with God for you! The treaty has been signed at the cross. Now, lay down your arms, and take up your cross, and follow Him.

A letter from "Regina"

> When I was about 6 years old, I came downstairs to my parents, in the living room, and I asked to be saved. But I can't really remember it very well, and I'm not sure I knew what I was doing. This bothered me for a very long time, so I also went forward at church to be saved when I was in high school. And, all along, I have said little prayers over and over to God, asking Him into my heart, or telling Him that I believe. And I've done it over and over and over again. And, because I feel no relief, I feel like I can't say that I believe Jesus' blood covers my sins. I know Jesus died on the cross, and that everyone's sin was on His shoulders (including mine). And I know it is only through Him that we are saved. But, at the same time, it's like I don't believe I was saved in my living room.

My response:

Regina, do you realize what you are saying? You are saying, "I have no problem with the salvation Jesus provided me on the cross, just the salvation He didn't provide me in my living room." There is no other salvation than the salvation Jesus provided by His death, burial, and resurrection. And as long as you look for any other, you will remain defeated.

All this time, Regina, you have known that Jesus' death for you was the way to heaven. But you are not resting in what you know Jesus did for you on the cross, because you are unsure of something He might not have done for you in your parents' home. So, because you are unsure about what happened in your parents' living room, then you are unsure if you are saved.

To overcome this, you must realize that your salvation is not something that happened in your parents' living room; it is something that happened to Jesus, when He took your sin and died in your place on the cross. By realizing this, since you are sure of what Jesus did on the cross, then you will be sure of your salvation. But when people think of their salvation as something they did on a certain day, they will often try to reassure themselves of their "salvation" by doing a number of things, such as: rededicating their lives, making a public profession of faith, joining the church, surrendering to preach, or being re-baptized.

This may give them a little comfort, but that comfort will eventually fade away. When it does, they will often come to the conclusion that they were never truly saved. And, having come to that conclusion, they may try to "get saved" again by doing the same things that didn't work for them the first time (repeating their prayer, re-surrendering their lives, etc.).

When this happens, the whole process will repeat itself, and those poor people will embark on a seemingly endless cycle of repeating prayers for salvation (each time trying to pray more sincere and intense than the last), and hoping at least one of those prayers will actually stick and get them saved. Sound familiar?

If they continue on this cycle, they may eventually feel like giving up, because they will think there must be something wrong with them or that God doesn't like them, because they can never get assurance that God has saved them, while everybody else they know seems to have that assurance. Of course, there is nothing wrong with them, and there is nothing wrong with you. Your solution is simple: Stop fearing what you doubt Jesus did in the living room, and start resting in what you know Jesus did at the cross.

33 SOME FINAL WORDS

It would be impossible for me to cover every topic, explain every scripture, or answer every question you may have in a single book. But, the good news is, I don't have to. You don't have to dot every "I" and cross every "T" before you can have full assurance of salvation.

The Devil wants you to think that you are odd and that your situation is a special case. He wants you to think that your situation is more difficult than everybody else's. Don't believe it. I once thought I was a special case, too. I remember telling God one day, "Lord, if I ever figured out my salvation, and if you ever use me for anything, it will be an absolute miracle, because I am so stupid."

The Devil wants you to spend your entire life reading books and listening to different sermons, trying to "nail down" your salvation. But, the truth is, your salvation was "nailed down" to the cross, and it's time for you to accept this. It's time for you to accept the fact that *"It is finished"*. And, if it is finished for Jesus, then it should be finished for you.

I once heard a preacher say, "Just because I don't understand electricity, doesn't mean I'm going to sit in the dark until I figure it out."

So true. You don't have to know how to wire a house to turn a light switch on, and you don't have to know all the mysteries of salvation to accept the gift of salvation. I know very little about air, but that doesn't prevent me from breathing it. To me, it is simple: I need air to live, so I take it freely and without hesitation.

Even so, you may still have unanswered questions about salvation, but they should not prevent you from accepting it. You

KNOWING I'M SAVED

need Jesus to live, so you should take Him freely and without hesitation. Perhaps you may be thinking, "But, I have read and heard things that seem to condemn me, and I fear I cannot have peace until I figure them out." Be not troubled, friend. For, peace doesn't come by figuring out what we *don't* know but by accepting the truth we *do* know.

Think of someone you know very well. It could be anybody—a friend, a relative, a coworker. Suppose I showed you two rooms. In the first room, you see the person you know. The room is well lit, so you are sure it's that person in the room.

Now I show you the second room. The second room is not well lit. It is dark, with just enough light to reveal a shadowy silhouette of a person inside. Coincidentally, you happen to notice that the person in the dark room is similar in size, shape, and stature to the person you know is in the lighted room.

Would it be reasonable for you to doubt the identity of the person, who you know is in the lighted room, because you don't know who's in the dark room? Of course not! Even if there were a hundred rooms, it would make no difference. Why? Because the people you don't know in the dark rooms can't change the truth of who you know is in the lighted room.

It's the same way with salvation. Don't doubt the truth you do know because of the things you don't. When you can see salvation so clearly in most verses of the Bible, don't let the things that are "sitting in the dark rooms" cause you to doubt the truth you know.

The person in the dark room can't change the truth of who you know is in the lighted room. Likewise, the scriptures you don't understand can't change the truth of those you do. Never doubt in the dark what God has shown you in the light.

Throughout this book, I've referred you to John 3:18. It applies here as well. In that verse, Jesus said, *"He who believes on Him is not condemned..."* Do you believe on Him? Are you relying on Jesus as your Savior? If so, the Bible says you are not condemned.

Acts 13:38-39 says, *"Therefore be it known to you, men, brothers, that through this man the forgiveness of sins is preached to you. And by Him all who believe are justified from all things..."* Do you believe the wonderful announcement of the *"forgiveness of sins"* that Jesus accomplished for you on the cross? If you do, you are justified (freed from guilt) from all things.

Ephesians 1:13 says, *"you heard the word of truth, the gospel of your salvation: in whom also after that you believed, you were sealed with that Holy Spirit of promise . . .* " Have you heard the word of truth, the gospel of your salvation? If you've read this book, you certainly have. And, having heard what Christ has done for you, do you now believe in Christ for your salvation? If so, when you believed, *"you were sealed with that Holy Spirit of promise"* (you were claimed by God and approved by God).

These are just a few promises God has shown you in the lighted room. So, if you know you believe on Jesus, then you know you have eternal life, and you need not fear those dark rooms that have been troubling you any longer.

Next, regardless of what Bible verse you read, always remember: scripture will never contradict scripture. If one verse of scripture clearly promises you eternal life but another appears to condemn you, then your interpretation of the more obscure verse is wrong. When you encounter this, trust what you do know, and wait on what you don't know. Do this, and you will find that some of the scariest verses in the Bible, once their true meaning is learned, may become your most cherished.

Trust nothing but the Word of God. Too often, I encounter people who are troubled about a scary sermon they've heard or somebody's testimony they've heard, which does not align with their own. Neither fret yourself over the words of men nor confide in them. Let the Word of God alone be your comfort as well as your conviction. Do this, and before long, you will be able to discern between truth and error in the words of men.

I once had a dog that was fiercely loyal to me. One day, my brother, who looks and sounds a lot like me, went into my backyard and called for my dog. At first, my dog was happy to see and hear my brother. She thought my brother was me. But, after she saw me standing next to my brother, she realized my brother wasn't me, and she immediately chased him out of my yard. This is how you should be toward everything you hear. No matter how legitimate something sounds, if it's not God's Word, chase it out of your yard.

Finally, a word of advice to those who have believed: It is a mistake to assume all doubts will be removed once you are saved. Pharaoh chased the children of Israel after they were free from Egypt, and the Devil will chase you after you are free from sin. After you are saved, there are three things you can always count on:

Number 1: You will always be you. After you're saved, you will still have all the crazy hang-ups you had before. You will have the same weaknesses, the same pitfalls, and the same peculiarities. By God's grace, you will overcome these in some measure. But, until you are changed at the rapture, you will continue to struggle with your sinful nature, and you will be prone to fall into the same old traps.

Number 2: The Devil will always be the Devil. After you are saved, you can always count on the Devil pulling the same old tricks he did before. And (trust me) he will pull some new ones, too. He is the Devil, and he will always be your enemy. So, you will still be you, and the Devil will still be the Devil, but . . .

Number 3: Jesus will always be Jesus, and the Word of God will never change! No matter what happens to you; no matter what mistakes you make; no matter what the Devil does or says to you, it can't undo who Jesus is and what Jesus has done for you.

Nothing can change the history of Calvary. Jesus died for your sins. It is written in the Bible, and that means your salvation is forever documented in the unchanging Word of God. The words, *"Christ died for the ungodly"* (Romans 5:6) shall forever be recorded in God's heavenly docket. And, because you have this unchanging pardon, you have an unchanging peace.

You are sinful; you are unholy; you are unreliable and prone to fall and disappoint your God. But Jesus *"is holy, harmless, undefiled, separate from sinners and made higher than the heavens"* (Hebrews 7:26). Though we change, He is *"the same yesterday and today and forever"* (Hebrews 13:8). As your high priest, Jesus stands ready to represent you before God. And, through the preaching of the gospel, God offers you the opportunity to be judged on Jesus' merit, instead of your own.

Once more, will you accept God's offer? Will you allow God to judge you no longer on the basis of who you are and what you have done but on the basis of who Christ is and what Christ has done for you? If so, you are saved.

Do not close this book, then, without resting the full weight of your confidence in the cross of Jesus Christ. Do this, and we shall meet in heaven.

RICHARD FULTON

ABOUT THE AUTHOR

Throughout parts of his childhood and into his young adult life, Richard Fulton struggled with recurring doubts about his salvation. His struggle reached a climax in 1994, as he neared the end of what had been, for him, a very long and difficult spiritual battle. Due to the fear and anguish he experienced, Richard determined that, if God ever brought him out of the confusion he was in, he would do what he could to help others who were in that same condition. Ultimately, God, in His grace, called Richard out of darkness into the marvelous light and peace found only in Jesus and his cross.

Richard is currently the senior pastor of Central Baptist Church, in Mabank, TX, and the founder of KNOWIMSAVED.COM. Richard has a Doctor of Theology degree from Andersonville Theological Seminary, where he teaches the course, "Evangelism in the Local Church."

Made in the USA
Middletown, DE
16 March 2024